W9-BSL-356

Dogs can teach us
to enjoy the ride.

Smile and your dog
smiles with you.

Friends are as important to dogs as they are to people.

Dogs are sometimes our
greatest listeners.

The

ULTIMATE

DOG
lover

The Best Experts' Advice for a Happy, Healthy Dog with Stories and Photos of Incredible Canines

Marty Becker, D.V.M.
Gina Spadafori
Carol Kline
Mikkel Becker

Health Communications, Inc.
HCI Books, the Life Issues Publisher
Deerfield Beach, Florida

www.hcibooks.com
www.ultimatehcibooks.com

On the Cover: Lilly, the wondermutt, is a coconut retriever (island dog)—a breed not recognized by the AKC but coveted by human companions. Christy Dove adopted Lilly from the Humane Society of St. Thomas (U.S. Virgin Islands) after she was found in the "bush" at four months old, having been severely beaten and abandoned. Today, Lilly is full of personality and prefers being dressed to going "naked," being carried, especially when she feels insecure, and playing and wrestling with her grandfather. Lilly doesn't realize that she is not a human child, and no one is about to burst her bubble. (Mom takes some responsibility for these self-image issues.) To contact Lilly, e-mail her at lilly@stjbigfish.com.

**Library of Congress Cataloging-in-Publication Data
is available through the Library of Congress.**

©2008 Marty Becker, Gina Spadafori, Carol Kline, Mikkel Becker
ISBN-13: 978-0-7573-0750-8
ISBN-10: 0-7573-0750-7

Publisher: Health Communications, Inc.
   3201 S.W. 15th Street
   Deerfield Beach, FL 33442-8190

R-09-08

Cover Design: Larissa Hise Henoch
Cover Photo: ©2007 Patrick Shannon
Photo Editor: Justin Rotkowitz
Interior Design: Lawna Patterson Oldfield

*We dedicate this book to every dog who
lavishes gifts on a human family.*

*To the families who make sure their dogs' health
and happiness are a priority.*

*To all members of the veterinary healthcare team
and everyone involved with animal treatment,
rescue, and rehabilitation.*

*To all healthcare providers who harness
the healing power of pets to improve
human health and well-being.*

*To the special love of dogs as celebrated
in stories, photographs, memories,
and heartfelt emotions.*

*And finally to God for the gift of animals and the
life-affirming bond we share with them.*

Is something "Ultimately" important to you? Then we want to know about it. . . .

We hope you enjoyed *The Ultimate Dog Lover*. We are planning many more books in the Ultimate series, each filled with entertaining stories, must-know facts, and captivating photos. We're always looking for talented writers to share slice-of-life true stories, creative photographers to capture images that a story can't tell, as well as top experts to offer their unique insights on a given topic.

For more information on submission guidelines, or to suggest a topic for an upcoming book, please visit the Ultimate website at **www.ultimatehcibooks.com**, or write to: Submission Guidelines, Ultimate Series, HCI Books, 3201 SW 15th St., Deerfield Beach, FL 33442.

For more information about other books by Health Communications, Inc., please visit **www.hcibooks.com**.

Contents

Teachers and Healers

Unconditional Love

Celebrating the Bond

Must-Know Info

Introduction

We love dogs.

It may seem today's canine craziness is new, but it's not. Dogs and people have always been intricately entwined, our ancestors and theirs, living and working together throughout the generations. And it wasn't just a working relationship: archaeologists have found fossilized evidence of ancient dogs curled up with ancient humans, suggesting a bond that was about more than just dogs helping us hunt for our food or control our livestock. We wanted them in our lives, and they wanted to be in ours, from the beginning.

Few of us today have sheep to herd, or sleds to pull, or need a dog to help bring home our dinner. And yet, dogs are more popular than ever. What gives?

Today our love of dogs is a new kind of partnership, one of companionship, and science has documented the benefits: Pets in general, and dogs in particular, are good for us in countless ways. They keep us busy, keep us from being lonely, and even help us stay healthier.

Those of us whose hearts are in this book are unabashed animal lovers. Animals are our lives and the work we have chosen—whether as veterinarians, writers, or photographers. We cannot imagine living without them. We love dogs in all sizes and shapes, love them from the first whiff of puppy breath to the last sad good-bye. We love the snuggles on the couch while watching TV, the bracing walks on a cool fall afternoon, the sharing of a joke or a secret or even a little bit of our dinner. Our dogs are always with us, in spirit even when they cannot be with us in person.

We know we are not alone in the appreciation of all things canine. Every dog lover knows dogs don't care who we are or what we look like. They love us, regardless.

And more. Dogs teach us, heal us, make us laugh, and break our hearts with their passing. At a time when maintaining human connections seems to be more difficult, a four-legged family member can ease the loneliness and help us connect with other people.

We understand the benefits of canine companionship because we live with dogs, love them, and care for and about them. Our lives are about helping others to find better, fuller lives with their pets. The strength of the human-animal bond and the growing importance of pets in our lives is why we wanted to do this book.

The very best experts—top veterinarians, trainers, behaviorists, and more—were tapped to provide expertise on all manner of canine topics, but we wanted much more. We knew dog lovers had stories of canine love, loyalty, laughter, rescue, and courage, and we knew we wanted to share them, along with pictures that are each worth more than a thousand words.

From thousands of submissions of stories and photographs, we have chosen the very best. The ones we loved, and the ones you'll love, too.

Celebrate the dog with us. Turn the page, and enjoy.

Acknowledgments

It takes a talented team working behind the scenes to make magic in a book happen. There are dozens of people, each with a specific niche, who brought *The Ultimate Dog Lover* from conception to creation to its place on your favorite booksellers' shelves.

Our biggest thanks goes to our dogs—past and present—for their patience while we learned how to love, nurture, and care for them and for letting us into their world.

Thank you to everyone who submitted stories or photographs for consideration. While we were only able to use a small portion of the thousands of stories and photographs that were sent in, we know that each word and photo came from a heartfelt place.

This book would not have been possible without the generosity of some of the world's top veterinarians, behaviorists, trainers, breeders, and other experts who have dedicated their careers to making life better for pets and people. You'll find all you need to know about these talented professionals following each of the "Must-Know Info" topics in which they shared their expertise.

We especially thank Peter Vegso, our publisher for our last eight pet books, who believes in us and supports us in a myriad of ways.

With Health Communications, Inc., (HCI) there is harmony, joy, trust, flexibility, excitement, experience, professionalism, candoism, and a shared love of both pets and people. We tip our hats in sincere appreciation and respect to every member of the HCI team whose efforts allow us to show off these books with pride!

We owe a huge amount of gratitude and love to our story editor, Cindy Buck, whose enormous talent and commitment are only rivaled by the beauty of her heart, mind, and spirit. Cindy, we couldn't have done it without you—nor would we have wanted to.

On a more personal level, we simply cannot do what we do without the support of our family and friends.

Marty wishes to thank his beloved wife, Teresa, son Lex, daughter Mikkel, and son-in-law Pat, for their love and support. The Becker family shares Almost Heaven Ranch in northern Idaho with a menagerie of four-legged family members—dogs, cats, and horses—that are a constant source of joy. Worthy of special mention is his colleague, mentor, and friend, Dr. R. K. Anderson, one of the cofounders of the Delta Society, a world-renowned veterinary behaviorist, and inventor, and the founder of ABRIonline.org.

Gina's love and appreciation goes out to her brother Joe, who is her very best friend, and her parents, Louise and Nino, her brother Pete, his wife, Sally, and their bright and talented children, Kate and Steven. Thanks to Christie Keith and Morgan Ong, friends who are really family. And of course, to all the animals who continue to teach the lessons of love and acceptance.

Carol thanks her husband, Larry, who is the love of her life and who not only makes it possible for her to spend all of her time writing and editing, but makes it all worthwhile. Thanks also to her wonderful stepchildren, Lorin and McKenna, and to her mother, Selma, brothers Jim and Burt, and sisters Barbara and Holly, and their families, for being her favorite people in the world. Big belly rubs and lots of w-a-l-k-s for dogs, Beau, Beethoven, and Jimmy-pop.

Mikkel foremost wants to thank God for his love and blessings. Her dearly loved husband, Pat, never ceases to make her laugh and keep her life full with his on-the-edge spontaneity and fun, while her children (pugs), Willy and Bruce, keep her entertained with their wrestling and cuddling. And special thanks to her family cheerleaders, who have shared her accomplishments and achievements: Marty, Teresa, Lex, Valdie, Rockey, Virginia, Joan, Pete, Mike, and Joanie, for their enduring love and support.

Marty Becker
Gina Spadafori
Carol Kline
Mikkel Becker

four-Legged Family Members

This Is True Love

By Bonnie West

Fur in my face: sweet, warm, soft. I roll over into the familiar dog smell and inhale deeply. Jockeying for prime space in the bed, I nudge him. He lifts his heavy head and he gives me "the look," before moving his old body and then settling deeply into my husband's pillow a few inches farther from my nose.

Beasley knows his master is away and the bed is ours. He knows that I don't mind the grit beneath us, shaken off as he lumbered up; knows I like the blankets scrunched and balled around us and the sheet tangled beneath us; knows I love the popcorny smell of his paws and his low, slumbering moans.

We are so bold, sharing the bed.

My husband is gone for two weeks. He is touring with the Minnesota Orchestra, and during this time there will be no savory smells in the kitchen, no bright and bleached laundry to fold, no spanking clean sheets. We are alone, the dog and I, and we come and go as we please. He drinks from the toilet. I leave the doors unlocked and the dishes in the sink. I call out for pizza, and the Big Pease and I, we share.

Oh, sometimes we miss the man. I miss him because I love

him, and no getting around it, after all these years, I'm used to him. Beasley misses him because he loves him, too—and he also misses the treats. When my husband is home, Beasewalldeen gets treats for going out, treats for coming in, treats for sitting, treats for lying down, treats for wagging his tail, treats for no reason. My husband's a soft touch. But Beasley and I, we don't let this "missing stuff" bother us. We are on vacation. We are free!

Some days we get in the car and drive for hours; we never tell anyone where we are going or when we are coming home.

We drive with my elbow sticking out one window and his muzzle out the other. I tell Bees-Knees my darkest secrets, my grandiose plans, and my little hopes. He thinks they are all terrific. I ask him how come he can stick his nose out the window at forty miles an hour, but go totally nuts, really whacko, if I blow in his face. I ask him if he really dreams about chasing rabbits. He nods and wags. The Beasy Beast licks my face, but I don't let him do it again. There are some things only the man can take. Our days of freedom and bliss fly by. We are happy romping and playing and doing our thing. But then, at the end of the second week, the house is a shambles, our stomachs ache from the junk food, and all at once, we both get sick of the fun. Again and again, Beasley jerks up, cocks his head hopefully, then collapses back down, disappointed at the sound of the wrong car.

He drags himself, hangdog, over to me, lays his head in my lap, and looks up accusingly, *What have you done, buried him in the backyard?*

"One more day," I say and pat my sad dog's head. But there is no consoling him. He's sick of the good life and wants me to go out there and dig him back up. I am a little hurt. My Beasty Boy loves me, but I am not the love of his life. I'm merely the stand-in, the good-time girl, the substitute. He misses his master and wants him back.

When the cab pulls up, the front door finally opens, and the man is home. Beasley flings himself against those familiar legs and leaps into waiting arms; he licks and cries and wags and whimpers for joy. And suddenly, I know: this is true love, a love so great that an old dog gladly gives up the pillows and blankets and sheets and sleeps, again, on the floor by the bed.

The Great Yaakie Mystery

By Isabel Bearman Bucher

Yaakie was an ever-curious, mischief-seeking personality in a big, fat, belly-to-the-ground dachshund body. He'd been bought as a companion for me when I was just a baby. As the years passed, he became, in equal measure, fatter, more independent, and less tolerant. He set his limits, and although he was slow to come to them, come to them he did. I still carry a scar on my thumb where he sank in his incisor when I pinched his yellow eyebrow spot with the two perfect feeler hairs once too often.

In the dead of our Connecticut winters, Yaakie would hurl himself off the front porch steps into the deep snow.

"Up periscope!" my brother, David, would squeal, anticipation bubbling in his throat.

Out of the snow would emerge two perfect points—nose and tail. He'd get to his business, points disappearing for a few seconds, then the periscope would swivel and zero in on the steps. He'd take a hulking leap, followed by a vigorous shake, and end with a whine for the "open sesame."

"He's a badger dog," I'd proudly announce, having read about his breed. "They're at home in tunnels!"

One year the "great Yaakie mystery" would show just how true to his breed he was.

Summers, David and I often dressed Yaakie in baby clothes and toted his plenteous personage around in a doll carriage, keeping him in there with bribes of food—usually a baby bottle filled with sugar milk—or sheer force, which didn't help his disposition. For this operation, we donned mittens. One day his bulk busted the doll carriage, and Nonno, our grandfather, wouldn't fix it. That left the red Flyer wagon, in which we'd go racing down the hills, one of us gripping him tightly, always ending with the crowning sideways-dump. Winters, he became a great sledder, and an even greater rider of old, flattened cardboard boxes that careened dizzily down the icy slopes behind our house. He'd sit up front and proud, clasped in our vicelike grips, with that Yaakie smile and ears flying out in victory Vs. I suspect height and speed were his passions because he himself had neither.

In 1942, Nonno bought a two-hundred-acre Vermont farm, and early that summer Mamma loaded us up for the first visit; Dad would come on weekends. When we turned up a steep dirt track to Nonna and Nonno's farm, Mamma laid on the horn. Nonna, desperate to see us, ran to a steep drop, high above, and waved a white sheet like crazy so we didn't take any wrong turns.

The farm had its limitations. When you cranked the wooden phone on the wall, half of Lyndonville was on the party line. And Nonno hadn't gotten around to the indoor plumbing yet, so when duty called in the middle of the night, David and I dragged Yaakie with us to the "outy," whose door sported a half-moon cutout surrounded by a few stars. Terrified, we always went together. One of us stood outside and whistled while the other went in, hauling an equally unnerved dog. We figured if something with claws, quills, or an up-tail scent-shooter lurked in that black abyss, Yaakie would sound first alert. He'd sit whining and shivering in the cramped, smelly space, his luminous eyes reflecting the moonshine that ribboned in through the cutouts in the door.

That was the summer we began the greatest game ever created by two kids: the hayloft jump. Of course, we included Yaakie. First, we stuffed him into a gunnysack with only his head hanging out. It was the only way we could get him up to the hayloft. Then grasping the slats of the hayloft ladder, David and I switched off front-end hauling or back-end shove jobs, goosing Yaakie's ample behind and sometimes accidentally letting his long nose hit the rungs. Yaakie endured this discomfort with stoic acceptance because of what he knew was coming. High in the loft, we twined our arms around each other with Yaakie wedged in between us. There would be that terrifying moment of truth, and then—*banzai!* The *ménage à trois* went flying into the dusty space, plunging down fifteen feet into the hay below. Yaakie was always first to wiggle out of the pile, while David and I lay in the deep hay, totally helpless, paralyzed and convulsed by spasms of laughter. With a howl, a bark, and a curl of his lips into that rakish smile, Yaakie would flail, heave himself around, tongue going in and out like a buzz saw as he panted, ready for another go—so many we lost count.

"Nonna!" I called one day. A Florentine-trained artist, she was painting a Vermont landscape, using the fine view of the surrounding countryside, with Sugarloaf Mountain in the distance.

"Yaakie's gone! He's been gone all day!"

"Ummm," she mumbled over the two oil brushes in her mouth. It was the usual adult response when they weren't interested in what you had to say.

"Nonna, he's gone." I began to cry. She took the brushes out, put down her palette, and turned to look at me with those wondrous dark eyes.

"Oh, *Dio mio*. Come. I dry your eyes," she singsonged. "He'll come back, *cara mia*. He's on holiday. You know that mischief bag."

But Nonna was wrong. Yaakie *was* gone. Who would know that best, but his two tormentors and joy makers?

For six days we searched the countryside. Nonno dragged out the rickety buggy, hitched up the old one-eyed horse, and off to the cow pastures we rolled, calling and calling.

No Yaakie.

We searched the forests; we searched down by the brook. We searched the nearby farms. We went over to the one-room country school, where a dog looking for a handout might smell lunches.

No Yaakie.

We asked everybody we met, traveling far from our farm. We put signs up in churches and Vermont country stores; we nailed them on the covered bridges. Later we went up and down the country roads looking for his body.

No Yaakie.

David and I cried ourselves to sleep. The adults tried to console us with candy and ice cream. Inconsolable, we walked around like a small traveling wake, shrouded in our beloved gunnysack.

Finally, Nonno clapped his hands in exasperation. Nonna refused to dry any more tears and went back to her easel. Momma stated that we were going to get something to cry for if we didn't stop. Dad did grief counseling, explaining doggie heaven. Nothing could change the sad truth: Yaakie was gone without a trace.

Days later, David and I were dragging the gunnysack by the barn when I suddenly stopped, squatted down, and listened intently. I rose like a shot, and began hollering.

"Nonna! Nonno! Hurry! I can hear him! He's under the barn!" I shrieked in breathless gulps.

"Yaakie! Yaakie!" David and I shouted. "Here, boy! Here!"

Faintly, came the sound of whining. Then there came a bit of a muffled yelp.

Nonno came with the shovel, Dad with the pick ax. For one hour, they pried at the rotten floorboards, dug up earth and rocks, and sweated, while we called and whistle-kissed, lending moral support. Yaakie kept up the whine and yelp cadenza, which added to the ongoing people opera, consisting of Italian bad words, orders, opinions, and insults hurled at the fatso.

"Eeza gonna come down, dat-a barn," predicted Nonna.

"*Dio Cristo*," mumbled Nonno. "Deez-a animal drive-a me crazy."

"Now, now, Papá," singsonged Momma.

"I don't know," Dad mumbled.

"Come on, Yaakie!" David and I cheered.

Soaked with perspiration, Dad and Nonno had to dig four feet down and over five. Nonna aimed the flashlight, while Nonno crawled in. He grabbed a tail, then a rump, and finally, out backed the two of them, completely covered with sweat and dirt. Yaakie's tongue was doing the buzz saw; his mouth was smiling.

He struggled out of Nonno's arms and began running in wild and crazy circles, around, around, around the yard, eight days skinnier, completely devoid of that low-slung belly—a free dog, at last. David and I came right behind, chasing, screaming, and laughing. He'd throw his head up and howl, then turn it sideways looking at us, finally planting slobbering tongue licks all over our faces. You never saw a happier dog.

We were over the moon, too. At last we knew where our ornery but adorable Yaakie had gone. He'd chased a badger down into a tunnel and couldn't back out over a rotted floor joist that collapsed into the hole.

Yaakie lived to be a very old dog. He never went near a hole again. He taught both of us to know when enough was enough, to seek and solve mysteries, and to believe that even if you're short and fat . . . you can fly.

The dachshund was developed to hunt badgers, but today is a favorite family pet.

Do dogs like kids better than kids like dogs? Probably a tie.

Ooh, yes,
scratch right there.

Table manners at the family dinner? Maybe not, but you have to give points for patience.

Many breeds and mixes get labeled as "pit bulls," but most of these dogs are stable, good-natured pets.

Clearly a case of puppy love.

Snuggle? Oh yeah,
I love to snuggle.

The beagle has always remained one of the most popular breeds.

The Ham Sandwich Summer

By Diane M. Ciarloni

I don't remember how old I was before I realized a beagle wasn't the only breed of dog in the world. As far as I was concerned, they provided everything anyone could want in a dog. Beagles are extremely smart and capable. Their primary negative quality is their hound-dog baying, which, admittedly, can drive a person crazy. Nose pointed skyward, mouth forming a tiny Cheerio-like circle, a mournful sound comes rising from the throat. Sometimes so much energy is expended that their front feet actually lift off the ground.

When I was growing up, we had a beagle named Duke who seemed to me more human than canine. I believe Duke saw himself that way, too. Nonetheless, my father, being a farmer, didn't believe in having animals in the house, so he built Duke a large doghouse in the backyard with a huge fenced-in pen. The doghouse was kept well-stocked with discarded blankets, which, as soon as the weather turned warm, Duke promptly hauled out onto the front porch Daddy had built for him.

That dog learned how to scramble onto the roof of his house and then launch himself onto the fence. He then hooked his feet in the wire fencing and scaled it, up one side and down the other, with the ease of the most agile trapeze artist. He was then free to go about his beagle business.

As soon as we figured out Duke's escape technique, Daddy installed boards at the top of the fence, all the way around the pen. Now the enclosure looked like Alcatraz. And Duke still found his way to freedom.

The beagle escaped nearly every night and always made a bee-line for the screened porch on the back of our house. Again using his multitalented paws, he opened the screen door and entered. The first thing he did was check Mama's old wringer-style washing machine. She sometimes put clothes in there in the evening, intending to wash them the next morning. If that were the case, Duke jumped in and made a comfortable bed. If not, he helped himself to the ratty sofa where Daddy sat to take off his dirty work shoes before going into the house. I don't think the washing machine or the sofa were any more comfortable than the pile of blankets in Duke's doghouse. I think he just wanted to be closer to his family, in case we needed him in the dark.

Duke started disappearing for a while every day, but we didn't mind that. You see, this was back in the days when most dogs ran loose around the countryside. Duke was a confident beagle. He knew his way around the area, and all the neighbors knew Duke, many by name and others by sight. That was a good thing, because the beagle harbored one extremely bad habit: he always walked smack down the middle of the road. Many times we saw cars stop for him or move to the edge of the road to accommodate his passage. Try as we might, we couldn't teach him differently.

I didn't pay much attention to Duke's absences until one day I happened to be in the yard and looked up just as Duke was turning into the driveway. There was something dangling from his mouth. It was . . . it was . . . a brown paper bag lunch. I removed it from his mouth (he didn't protest) and opened it. Inside was a piece of cake and two ham sandwiches.

"Duke, where in the . . . " Before I finished the question, a fellow in work coveralls came striding down the driveway, calling, "Hey! Hey! Is that your dog?"

Oh, no. There was a factory across the road from our house, and this man looked to be one of the workers.

"Yes, sir," I answered. Duke turned, positioned himself next to me, and sat against my legs.

I was relieved when the man's mouth turned into a smile—a very small smile, but still a smile. "He's been coming over to the factory for about a month now and stealing lunches. Sometimes he steals one, eats it on the spot, and then steals another one to take with him."

"But how does he get to them?" I asked. "Where do you leave them?"

"We have a small coat room," he explained, "before you go into the main part of the factory. We leave our lunches there."

"How do you get into the room from the outside?" I asked. I felt as if I were reconstructing the scene of a crime.

"A screen door," he said.

The mystery was solved. There wasn't a screen door within five hundred miles that Duke couldn't handle.

"Did you look to see what kind of sandwich was in the bag?" the man asked.

"Ham."

He started laughing. "He never steals the bags with bologna in them. It's always the ham."

I held out the rescued bag. "Would you like to take this back to . . ." I looked at the name written on the outside, ". . . Sam?" Without waiting for an answer, I said, "I can try really hard to keep him at home."

The man shook his head. "Sam needs to take off a few pounds, so let the beagle keep the sandwich. As far as keeping him home, well, we're kind of used to seeing him. We'd probably miss him." Actually, Duke didn't need the lunch any more than Sam. Weeks of ham sandwiches had added a few pounds he didn't need.

It was Duke's bad habit of walking down the middle of the road that took him from us. It was a summer afternoon. He was returning from a visit to my cousin's house and was just a few feet from turning into the driveway when a car seemed to come from the proverbial nowhere. Duke didn't stand a chance.

It was amazing how many people came by during the next week and offered their condolences. It was amazing because ours was a farming community and such grief over a dog wasn't 100 percent seemly.

Then, one day, a group of coverall-clad guys from the factory knocked on our door. One handed me a brown paper bag. Inside was a picture of Duke. One of the men had captured him on film with a hefty ham sandwich hanging from his mouth. They'd blown it up and put it in a frame. I looked up to thank them but the leader held up his hand.

"He was a good beagle," he said. "We'd give up all our lunches to have him back."

Yeah. He was a good beagle. I wasn't ten years old yet, but I knew surviving this grief meant I'd be able to survive anything life sent my way. And it's true. I'm still here, and to this day, I can't eat a ham sandwich without smiling.

Mr. Chip

By Marianne Allen

My husband, Robert, and I have learned that it works best for us to always have three dogs: an old one, a middle-aged one, and a young one. That way, as the older dog gets hard of hearing, dim-sighted, and stiff, the two younger ones have each other and leave the older dog in peace.

But once, due to a genetic short-circuit, our middle dog, a Queensland heeler named Smidget, died suddenly at the age of eight, leaving us heartbroken and with a set of mismatched book-ends, a young dog and an old dog. We began looking for a dog to fill the hole in the middle. We loved Smidget so much that we set our sights on another female Queensland heeler.

One afternoon, a few weeks later, Robert came home from work and told me he'd gone to the animal shelter that day and met a wonderful dog. "It's a he, and he's not a Queensland heeler," he explained. "He's an Australian shepherd. But he's the right age—six years old." Looking at my husband's face, which was lit with excitement, I knew we'd found our third dog.

The next day, while Robert was at work, I went to the shelter myself. I told them I had come to adopt the red merle Australian shepherd my husband had seen the day before. While one of the shelter staff went to get him, another told me his story.

The lady who'd brought the dog in was elderly, and her husband was in poor health. The couple had adopted him as an eight-week-old pup but couldn't care for him anymore. They'd named him Cocoa Chip, but the shelter workers called him Chip.

Chip had been at the shelter for a month and a half. The old woman phoned every day to ask if he'd found a new home, but so far there had been no one interested in such an old dog. As the weeks passed, Chip had become so depressed that he'd almost starved himself to death. The shelter staff, unable to comfort him, had reluctantly scheduled a date to put him down if he didn't improve.

When the door opened, I got my first look at our new dog. His coat was a reddish-brown, almost the same color as my own hair, with red and white speckled patches on his chest, legs, and ears. His eyes were a beautiful chocolate brown. Even in his distressed state, there was something truly gentle and sweet about him.

He looked around, his ears perked expectantly, but when he didn't see anyone he recognized, he drooped. At my call he came over to me, sniffed at my clothes, and let me pet him. He responded politely to my friendly tone of voice, but clearly he wasn't excited. His air was neutral, subdued, and sad.

I filled out the paperwork, and when the shelter was satisfied that I could provide a good home for Chip, they let me adopt him. Before we left, I asked them to give my number to the old lady who'd brought Chip in, so she could find out how he was doing.

In the car, Chip cried the whole way home. I tried to reassure him, but he wouldn't be comforted. He didn't know where he was going, and his most recent car ride—to the shelter—hadn't ended well for him.

When we arrived at the house, I brought the other dogs out to meet their new pack member. The older dog, a white-faced golden retriever, did some perfunctory sniffing and then padded off to find a place in the sun to snooze. The younger dog, Teaka, a two-year old Queensland heeler, was more interested, and sensing a new playmate, pranced around Chip, tail wagging enthusiastically. Chip responded in kind, showing the first sign of animation I'd seen in him.

I showed Chip around the house, pointing out the water bowl, food dishes, and dog beds, and then we walked out into the back-yard, which is large and fenced and ends in steep hill covered in periwinkles and oak trees. I told him that this was his yard and he could roam about however he wished. To demonstrate this, I unclipped his leash.

He stood still, his eyes opened wide. He looked all the way up the hill, then he looked at me, and his expression seemed to say, "You've got to be kidding. This is all *mine?*"

I told him, "Chip, welcome to your new home. You'll stay here forever, and we'll take as good care of you as we know how."

He looked again at the hill and at me and then an honest-to-God smile appeared on his face. You could almost see the tension drain from him.

I left him to explore his new kingdom.

Later, when my husband came home, we went looking for our

new family member. He wasn't in the house or in the front yard, and he wasn't on the front porch with the other dogs. We rounded the corner of the house and saw him, lying on the back stoop, his paws crossed, surveying his hill contentedly. That became his favorite place. From that moment on, we always knew where to find Chip.

Because of his gentle dignity, Cocoa Chip became Mr. Chip. This wonderful dog lived with us for almost ten more years. He and young Teaka became inseparable, playing together for hours until they dropped from exhaustion, and then curling up next to each other to nap. I called Teaka his girlfriend.

I had regular phone conversations with the old lady who'd brought Chip to the shelter, filling her in on his progress, but I didn't take him back to see her for about three months. I wanted him to know that we were his family and not to be confused.

The day of our visit, I decided to bring Teaka along as my ace in the hole. If Mr. Chip took it into his head to stay with the old couple, I knew I'd be able to entice him to leave by walking out of the door with Teaka.

When we arrived at his old home, he knew exactly where to go. As we walked up the path to the door, I could see why he'd been so excited about the big yard. Here he'd had a small square of lawn, with a doghouse taking up most of that space. Except for walks on a leash with the old woman, this had been the extent of his adventures in nature.

The reunion was a joyful one. Mr. Chip ran up to the old woman, licking her and whimpering excitedly, as she kissed and hugged him right back. But after a few minutes of this, when the first rush of emotion was spent, Mr. Chip came over and sat beside me, his message clear: this is my new mom.

I looked anxiously at the old woman, afraid that she might be hurt. Her eyes were filled with tears, but they were happy ones. She smiled at me and said, "Every day I asked God to find the right home for my Cocoa Chip. Now I can see that my prayers have been answered and that he is truly happy with his new life."

Mr. Chip was happy, and he made us happy as well. He played his role as the middle dog admirably, providing not only the balancing energy but also the heart at the center of our family. Later, when he became oldest dog, his tenure as patriarch was marked with a calm and steady devotion to us that never wavered. Though his path to our home wasn't a direct one, I have no doubt that Mr. Chip's coming to us was meant to be.

Operation Puppy Love

By Rinda Pope as told to Carrie Pepper

When my eighteen-year-old son, Alex, first joined the Army, I wanted to shake him and say, "Don't go." But I'd always tried to support him, and I didn't want to hold him back from something he truly wanted to do.

After he was deployed to Iraq, Alex and I kept in touch through his MySpace page. One of the things Alex wrote about was making friends with a dog the soldiers had trained for base protection. My son had always loved dogs. He'd grown up with a seventy-pound German shepherd named KC, who'd been devoted to him. When the dog on the base had puppies, Alex told me that he and the rest of the unit were looking after them. From the way he described the puppies, I could tell they were like little pieces of home for the soldiers—something to love.

Understandably, Alex had other things on his mind besides keeping in touch with his mother. But his platoon buddies also had MySpace pages, and, eager for more news about Alex and his life in Iraq, I started visiting them daily. One day I saw a picture posted of Alex and another soldier holding two of the puppies. I learned the other soldier was SPC Matt Alford, one of the men in Alex's platoon. I sent him an e-mail about the puppy picture and asked if he was a friend of my son's. He wrote back that he was, and we began corresponding regularly.

Matt became like my adopted son. He was always so open and willing to give me updates about what was happening there. When I felt worried because I hadn't heard from Alex in a while, I'd send Matt a message. He'd bang on the thin trailer wall that separated their rooms and yell, "Varela, your mom's online and says hi!" Alex would yell back, "Tell her I say hello and that I love her."

From time to time, I'd hear more about the puppies, who by then had grown into young dogs. One of them, a female named Bradley Position (after a Bradley tank), or BP for short, used to walk with Alex's platoon when they were out on patrol, as if she were protecting them.

Alex came home to California on leave at the end of January, just in time to celebrate his nineteenth birthday. During his "eighteen days on the ground" (eighteen days of vacation plus travel time), he had a great time visiting with family and friends. We barbecued and played video games together, and Alex spent some time with his Dad in Nevada. The day I sent him back to Iraq was one of the hardest days for me. I wanted to keep him at home so badly, but I knew he had to go.

That was the last time I saw him. Alex was killed May 19, 2007, when his Bradley armored vehicle was bombed by an improvised explosive device.

The devastation and profound sense of loss I felt at losing my son is something only those who have shared that pain can fully understand. A bit of my heart and soul lived and died with Alex, and while I was not alone in my grief, it was terribly lonely. I kept in touch with Matt after Alex's death. He, and the rest of the platoon, were always there for me and a source of comfort during that deeply painful time.

When I received Alex's possessions, I found a whole stack of photos of Alex and BP. I was so moved; looking at the pictures, I could tell that this dog had been special to my son. Knowing how she had stuck by the soldiers, even in the middle of the war zone, made her special to me as well. I asked Matt about her and learned that she was pregnant. Then, a few weeks later, in the beginning of November, I received an e-mail from Matt saying, "The puppies were born last night!" There were five puppies in the litter, but only one little female survived. They named her DJ after one of the guys in the unit, because both of them loved to eat!

That's when Matt had the idea to send DJ to me. BP was part of the unit and had to stay, but Matt wanted me to have her puppy. Matt would never take credit for Operation Puppy Love. He always said it was the work of the whole platoon, and I truly believe that. They didn't have much time because they would be leaving Baghdad within weeks, but somehow they made it happen.

When I think about what it took to get this puppy to American soil, I'm amazed they pulled it off. They did a lot of networking, and one of Alex's officers contacted Gryphon Airlines, the only commercial airline flying out of Baghdad. The airline's vice president got onboard from the beginning. He was so excited to help that he even e-mailed me personally to keep me informed of their progress. An embedded photographer attached to the unit took photos of the operation. I don't know how they managed to get a kennel, but the pictures that show two-month-old DJ being loaded onto the plane are proof that they did. They also hooked up with BlackFive, a military blog, that helped coordinate an escort for DJ from Baghdad to Kuwait and then on to Washington, D.C.

To this day, I don't know how much Operation Puppy Love cost the guys in the platoon—and they won't tell me. But I know how much they make, and it's barely a living wage, especially for the ones with families of their own. Sending DJ is just one example of the kindness and generosity they showed me in those dark days after Alex's death. Focusing on the progress of DJ's journey gave me something to think about other than my grief.

DJ arrived at Dulles International Airport in early January. The animal transportation service I found told me the cross-country trip would take about ten days. While they were on the road, I got daily reports from the driver/handler.

Word of Operation Puppy Love spread through the Internet and became national news. When DJ arrived at my house on January 16, 2008, it was quite a show. People were everywhere—in the front yard, along the sidewalk, and out on the street. Members of Rolling Thunder, the motorcycle group that travels the country to honor veterans and fallen soldiers, came over four hundred miles to stand in honor, along with the Patriot Guard Riders.

The moment approached for me to finally meet DJ. I was nervous. All these people were watching, including a local television crew. *What if DJ doesn't like me?* I thought.

As it turned out, I had nothing to worry about. When the driver put the wiggling, black-and-white puppy in my arms, she immediately started licking my face and wouldn't stop. The crowd broke into cheers as I hugged the little dog to my chest, tears streaming down my face.

After everyone left and the confusion and excitement of the day quieted down, DJ and I went out to the backyard. We'd both been through so much, and even though we couldn't communicate with words, our bond was strong. As I sat stroking her sleek coat, she showered me with puppy kisses. It seemed so natural to have her; it was like she'd always belonged to me.

Today it feels as though we were meant to be together. Having DJ with me helps to soothe the pain, at least a little. I feel as if I'm sharing something with Alex and that a small piece of my heart is being healed with every wag of her tail. She's such an affectionate dog and loves attention. Matt told me that the soldiers spoiled her over there; they treated her like a queen, sharing their chicken and rice with her, and giving her treats. She'd always had a buddy sitting with her or taking her out on patrol.

I think DJ's story says a lot about our soldiers in Iraq. The love my son and his unit had for these dogs gave them something to hold on to, and they generously shared that gift with me when I needed it most. I know Alex would have been glad that this sweet, rambunctious puppy made it here to be with me. It was a small victory, something going right against all the odds.

A New York Love Affair

By Harris Bloom

Two and a half years ago, when my live-in girlfriend, Bronwen, wanted a dog, I tried to convince her that it wasn't a good idea. Not only did we both work full-time, but I'd never had a dog. Hermit crabs were the only pets I'd been allowed as a kid, due to allergies. (Mine, not theirs.)

"Please?!?" she beseeched.

I stood my ground.

She batted her baby blues.

I held firm.

She extended her lower lip, pressed her palms together, fingers pointing skyward, and begged.

As tough as it was, I wouldn't give in.

This scene was replayed biweekly for over a month. Her lower lip must've been very sore. Sometime in the second month, no longer able to think clearly, I made a tactical mistake.

I asked, "If we were to get a dog, what kind of dog would you want?"

And that was that.

We headed out to the city's animal shelters to make some homeless doggy's day. Given our postage stamp–size Manhattan apartment, we had to get a small dog, but they were at a premium at the shelters, always snatched up as soon as they arrived. The few we saw had "issues" and would need more time and attention than our jobs allowed. We kept checking back, but no little dogs. So, we finally decided we had to buy one.

Bronwen had grown up with Yorkshire terriers and wanted to continue the family tradition. Specifically, she desired a "Paris Hilton Special"—one of those adorable pups that weigh about six pounds and can be carried around in a bag—in fact, *have* to be carried around in a bag so they don't get squashed.

I can't say I was thrilled. I pictured myself walking this "rat on a leash," explaining to everyone I passed that li'l Tinkerbelle was my girlfriend's dog. And then there was the price.

"How much are they?" I asked her.

"A couple thousand."

"*Dollars?!*"

"That's what my mom's cost."

"Two-thousand dollars? For a dog? Maybe we should check a few more shelters."

"Please?!?"

"Well, lemme see if we can get one cheaper."

An Internet search led to several Yorkie sites, where prices ranged from $1,000 to $4,000. Then I found one that only charged $750 for a purebred Yorkie. Two subways, a bus, and $850 later (we bought a cage and some toys), and we had a new member of our household: one Stewie Robinson Bloom.

It would make a better story if I could say I didn't take too kindly to Stewie's intrusion in my life, and complain about how

I viewed his very existence as an inconvenience, until slowly but surely I came to love him. But that's not what happened.

Stewie owned me from day one. I didn't mind when he peed on the carpet. I didn't mind when he used my socks as a chew toy. I didn't mind when he ate a twenty-dollar bill that had fallen to the floor. (Okay, I did mind that a little.) Most of all, I didn't mind when we realized that he wasn't even a Yorkie.

Our first clue was his ears. While Yorkie ears are perpetually up, as though listening intently to every last word, Stewie's ears were floppy, framing the sides of his head. Second was his nose, which protruded like a German shepherd's. Yorkies, of course, have button noses that complete their teddy-bear faces.

But the real giveaway was his size. Greg, the breeder had told us that Stewie would max out at six pounds, but by the time we'd had him for two months, he was already six pounds. The only way he was going to "max out" at that weight was if we put him on the Atkins diet and stuck him on a treadmill every day.

"We have the only $750 mutt on the Upper West Side," I joked, thinking, this is why you're supposed to check out the breeder before you buy. But to be honest, not only didn't I care, I was quietly thrilled. At a whopping twenty pounds when fully grown, Stewie was a "man's dog," with an outsized personality to match his oversized frame. He was a favorite at the dog run and a rock star in the neighborhood.

"Stewie!" We'd hear adults and children shout as I walked him. No one knew my name, of course, only his. I beamed with pride, even though I couldn't really take credit for his DNA.

Bronwen wasn't quite as thrilled. Though she loved Stewie,

too, she had wanted, and paid for, a six-pound Yorkie. When our vet told us that we shouldn't let the breeder get away with such deception, Bronwen took action: she made me call Greg.

"Um, hi, Greg?"

"Yes?"

"Yeah, hi, this is Harris Bloom. I, umm, we, that is me and Bronwen, we, umm, bought Stewie, well, a Yorkie, from you about two months ago?"

"Of course, hi. I remember! How are you guys doing?" he cheerfully asked. This was going to be harder than I thought.

"We're good, thanks. One thing though: I don't think the puppy you sold us is a Yorkie."

"Why do you say that?"

"Well, his ears haven't risen, his face isn't normal for a Yorkie, and he's already bigger than what you said he will weigh as an adult."

His voice suddenly became measured, like a doctor who has to deliver bad news. "Harris, there are several different kinds of Yorkies."

"Well, that may be true, but this isn't one of them."

"I'm sure it is. I've been selling Yorkies for ten years, so believe me when I tell you, I know Yorkies."

"Dude, if the dog you sold me is a Yorkie, then I'm a Chihuahua."

We continued in this vein for a while, with a steady rise in blood pressure, till Greg suddenly caved.

"Whether he is or isn't a Yorkie, I do want you to be happy. Tell you what, how about I just give you $200 back?"

Not really wanting to bother with filings or small claims court, I said, "Deal," and changed my running joke to "We have the only $550 mutt on the Upper West Side."

Things went beautifully for the next two years. Stewie and I would go to the dog run where he would play with the other dogs or fetch his favorite ball for hours. And then we'd go home where he'd immediately bring me his indoor (that is, nonsqueaky) ball.

Bronwen didn't have as much time to spend with him as I did. While my accounting job was strictly nine to five weekdays, Bronwen's work as a hairstylist meant long days and some weekends as well. But when she was home, we were a cozy threesome. It was the perfect life.

But unfortunately, over time, things started to change. What was cute and irresistible at the beginning began to grow tiresome. Though I had loved making sacrifices at first, gradually it became less of a joy. The constant demand for my attention, and the whining when I couldn't give it, got old. Finally, I had to admit to myself: it just wasn't that much fun, and I couldn't really see the point in continuing.

So Bronwen and I broke up. (You didn't think I was talking about me and Stewie, did you? Not for all the chew toys in Manhattan!) To be honest, if not for Stewie, we probably would've broken up much sooner. Neither one of us wanted to give up Stewie, but in the end, Bronwen admitted that he was really my dog all along, and that I should have him.

I thought that was very gracious of her, and I felt a little guilty, until one day recently when I caught a glimpse of her walking on the other side of the street. I was in a hurry and didn't want to stop to make small talk, but I did notice she had a bag slung over her shoulder. And peeking out of that bag was a six-pound Yorkie. I was glad to see she had someone to live happily ever after with, too.

Taking a Chance on Chance

By Lila Guzman

On Valentine's Day, 2001, we lost Sammy, our mixed-breed dog. We felt blessed to have had him for fourteen years and cherished our time with him. Still, we mourned his loss and knew that he would be hard to replace.

One day, several months later, I got a cryptic call from my husband, Rick. "There's something you've got to see," he said. He gave me directions and asked me to come as soon as possible.

I drove to a nearby town and found myself pulling into the parking lot of the local Humane Society. My ten-year-old son, Daniel, was pacing back and forth on the sidewalk. I had barely gotten out of the car when he grabbed my hand and dragged me into the animal shelter. He led me to the dog section where cages were stacked one on top of the other.

"Look, Mom!" Daniel said, gesturing to one on the bottom.

I hunched down and looked inside. There sat the sorriest-looking puppy in the pound, paws down. He didn't do anything cute and endearing, nothing that would have made me say, "That's the dog for us!" He just huddled in the back of the cage, looking terrified, staring at us with mournful eyes, and flinching at every sound. The medium-size puppy had a scruffy coat, unat-tractive ears, and a scrawny, rodent-like tail.

Animal Control had found him on a greenbelt. They had no way of knowing how long he had been by himself. The workers at the shelter had given him the temporary name of Reesie because his coloring reminded them of a Reese's Peanut Butter Cup.

Why my son picked him was beyond my comprehension.

I focused on the cage door. A handwritten note in big block letters read "Vocal Puppy." Great! Just what we needed: a barker. The neighbors would love him.

"Are you sure you want that one, Daniel?" I asked.

There was no need for an answer. His face glowed with pure joy.

I had seen that expression many times before when Daniel played with Sammy. Just like "Vocal Puppy," Sammy had come from the pound. He'd been a boxer-chow mix, if the tag on his door was to be believed, but everything about him had suggested otherwise. He'd had the characteristic square head of a pit bull. And when we got home with him, we soon learned that he would climb a tree to go after a toy and would hold onto a sock in his mouth and never let it go—no matter how hard you tugged. Whatever his breed, Sammy was the dog that my son had grown up with, and they had been best buddies.

Now, looking at "Vocal Puppy" and at Daniel's shining face—and that of his partner in crime (his dad)—I knew we had found our newest family member.

"Okay," I said. "Let's see how he behaves with us."

With the aid of a staff member, the three of us moved into a private room with Reesie.

Right away, the puppy found my husband's shoestrings and untied them. Rick retied them. The puppy immediately grabbed the ends and pulled again. Sighing in exasperation, my husband tied them again.

This went on until Rick gave up and fished his keys from his pocket. "Here, puppy. Play with these." He threw them. Reesie chased the key ring, picked it up in his mouth, and brought it back. He dropped it at Rick's feet and barked. If he could have talked, he would have said: "Throw it again, mister!"

Rick did—over and over. Daniel took up the game, and the puppy wore himself out playing fetch.

We had almost decided that this was our dog, when for no apparent reason, he let out a growl and attacked Daniel's pant leg. He grabbed the cuff and shook it back and forth.

I gave Rick a concerned look.

Then the puppy started barking at Daniel and gave his hand a puppy nip.

"I don't know if this is going to work out, Daniel," I said, worried about the sudden show of aggression.

"Please, Mom?" my son begged. "He's just a baby. He doesn't know anything yet."

"Will you take him to puppy kindergarten?" I asked.

"I sure will!" he said.

"Puppies can be a lot of work. You'll have to socialize him. We can't have a dog that bites."

"I'm willing to take a chance on him." Suddenly, Daniel's face brightened. "That's the name for him! Chance!"

So, we paid the adoption fee, stopped by the pet store for all the accoutrements we needed, and set up an appointment with the family vet for Chance's first physical exam.

That was seven years ago. Chance has turned out to be one of the best dogs we have ever had. "Vocal Puppy" grew up to become "Vocal Dog." When he senses a threat, the fur rises in a ridge on his back, and he barks. Every weekday at 4:45 PM, a different kind of sound comes out of him, he woofs with excitement, and his tail wags so hard that his whole body twists back and forth. Somehow he knows when Daniel has gotten off the school bus a block away and is walking up the street. Chance has become Daniel's best buddy, just as Sammy was.

Chance's scrawny tail eventually fluffed out and now curls up and over his back to make a lovely finishing touch, his only redeeming physical feature. Otherwise, with his scraggly ears, his ungainly body, and a coat that's just a mass of ratty, tufted fur, Chance is still incredibly ugly. However, his complete devotion to Daniel makes him one of the most beautiful dogs I have ever known.

A boy and his dog, no
better companions.

Most dogs are always
up for a ride.

This flat-coated retriever is enjoying a game of fetch.

Whatever you're doing,
your dog wants to know.

This Shetland sheepdog is
a captive audience.

If you yawn in front of your dog, don't be surprised if he yawns back—it's contagious.

The handsome Doberman is sensible, smart and friendly, but always prepared to protect his loved ones.

Who says dogs and
cats can't be friends?

Everybody Loves Lacy

By Linda Newton

W e hadn't been in our new house for more than two days when my daughter Sarah reminded me that she and her brother had been promised a puppy when we got to the new place, and this feisty four-year-old wasn't about to let any grown-up forget a promise. Realizing I would get no peace until I fulfilled my bargain, I told her that after lunch the whole family would head to the pound to pick out a puppy.

While I was still chewing the last bite of my sandwich, Sarah was off the stool and getting coats for herself and her two-year-old brother, Jacob. We all piled into the car, and my husband smiled over his shoulder at the two kids in the backseat chattering away about what kind of dog they would bring home.

The minute we walked in the door of the animal shelter I realized it had been a mistake to take two preschoolers into a room with so many adorable choices. Dogs were barking, crying, and jumping in their cages, and my kids were yelling, "I want this one," about every puppy in the place. I was just about to give up and come back another time when I spotted her—a little handful of black and white fluff. The sign on the pen read "Terrier-Poodle

Combination," but her true breed mixture was anyone's guess. All I knew was that in the midst of all of that commotion, she sat sweetly back on her hind legs with her tail wagging, smiling from ear to ear. With a precocious four-year-old girl and a boy heading into his terrible two's, I needed a calm, sweet dog. The attendant scooped her up and brought her out to us, and the entire family was hopelessly in love before ten minutes had passed.

By the time we were home, Sarah had decided on the name Lacy. I thought it fit her perfectly, and from then on Lacy fit our family perfectly. She went everywhere with us, riding in the car like a champ. Whether it was the meter reader or the paperboy, anyone who met her commented on how sweet she was. She even let the kids put baby clothes on her, a game I unsuccessfully tried to discourage.

"Mom, can Lacy watch TV with us?" the kids would ask each morning. Lacy would join them as they piled onto the beanbag chair. The kids would watch *Sesame Street,* and Lacy would watch the kids to see if they dropped any of the snacks they were eating. She wouldn't dream of taking food from their hands, but if it hit the ground, it was hers! When one of her kids was sick, Lacy would park herself on the feverish child, and they would rest so wrapped up together it was hard to tell where one left off and the other began. She always seemed to bring them comfort.

When our family was joined by another child, Lacy was just as good-natured toward Ashley, our new baby girl. I couldn't always hear the baby cry in our large house, but Lacy could. She would circle my heels, and I would know it was time to check the crib. As Ashley grew, so did Lacy's patience. It's hard to teach a toddler to be gentle. Lacy must have known that because she patiently tolerated all of the baby's clumsy attempts at showing love.

We didn't just add people to the household; we added pets as well. We adopted a golden Lab mix that needed a home. And when we moved to a home in a remote area, surrounded by miles of undeveloped land, we brought two feral cats to keep down the critter population. It took weeks to train the Lab not to chase or intimidate the poor cats, but not Lacy. She was their best friend right from the start. She let them drink from her water bowl and sleep on her dog bed, and they let her lick cat food out of their fur.

The kids grew up, and Lacy grew old. Still, when they drove their cars up our long driveway coming home from school, Lacy would rush to greet them, even when her arthritis made it hard for her to get off the porch. As her condition worsened, we spent a lot of time at the vet's office, trying to find the right medication to ease her pain.

On one of those visits, I questioned the doc, "There are times now when Lacy seems disoriented. I know she has suffered some hearing loss, but there seems to be more to her behavior than just that. Am I imagining things?"

Her reply was unexpected. "No, Linda, you're not. Dogs can get a form of dementia," she said. "It's hard to know if that's happening, but I would suggest that you keep her in for the most part. She could wander off and forget how to come home, especially on all that land around your house."

The kids that Lacy used to cuddle were all teenagers now, so that night at dinner I recruited their help. "We can't let her go outside unless somebody goes out with her," I instructed. They all agreed to watch out for their beloved old pooch. And they did, until one bustling Thursday night. The house was full of their friends who were hanging out until Youth Group started at church later that night. Kids were coming and going from every door. Just as the last kid left, I realized that Lacy wasn't in the house. By then it was dark, so my husband and I grabbed flashlights and looked all over the hillside. We called her for hours, even though I doubted that she could hear us. At midnight we gave up our search and decided we'd have better odds during the light of day.

The next morning the entire family joined in the search. We combed the countryside until the kids had to be at school and we had to be at work, but to no avail. That night I kept checking the porch, hoping to see Lacy resting there on her doggy bed and worrying when I didn't.

Saturday brought its usual chaos in a house full of teenagers. Sarah had to be dropped off at work, while Jake was heading out for music practice, and Ashley needed me to pick up a friend who was spending the day with her. As I went out to start the car, I couldn't believe my eyes. Walking up the long driveway was Lacy, alive and well, with the two feral cats flanking each side of her. The two cats nudged and rubbed against her, guiding her up the driveway, coaxing her toward home.

"Kids, come quickly!" I called. "You have to see this!" I needed witnesses. I wasn't sure I believed what I was seeing myself!

One by one, my children lined up behind me, wide-eyed and open-mouthed. We stood there silently until the three animals had made their way up onto the porch and were fiercely lapping up water. "They had their own personal *Incredible Journey*," Jake commented, remembering an old Disney movie we had watched over and over when he was younger.

"I needed you to see this because I knew you wouldn't believe me if I told you," I said.

"We wouldn't have, for sure," Ashley remarked. "It's just too amazing!"

Sarah shook her head and summed up what we were all thinking, "Everybody loves Lacy. Even the cats!"

Sweeter Than Ice Cream

By Dallas Woodburn

Kerr's Sweet Shop was a small, old-fashioned ice cream parlor located in the pleasant little town of Urbana, Ohio. In business since 1910, Kerr's always had a relaxed, well-worn atmosphere, as comfortable as a favorite pair of jeans.

Urbana is such a tiny town that most everyone knows everyone else. As a matter of fact, they usually don't just know *you;* they know your father and grandfather and possibly even your great-grandfather, too.

In the late 1930s, when my own grandfather was a young boy, he visited Kerr's quite often on his way around town with his dog, a boxer he called Gar. Gar, short for Gargantua, was named after the mythical giant. A large puppy, he'd grown to be a big dog—"Ninety-seven pounds of pure muscle," the boy would proclaim proudly.

Whenever he visited the ice cream parlor, which was almost daily in the summer, the boy always ordered two ice cream cones—a chocolate one for himself, and a vanilla one for Gar. The boy, a confirmed "chocoholic," felt bad that Gar always had to settle for vanilla, but he knew that chocolate is dangerous for dogs. Besides, Gar didn't seem to mind; he wagged his stubby tail gleefully when the boy held out the vanilla cone for him to lick as they sat together on the steps outside. The boy often said, half-seriously, that if they could find a way to harness the energy of that tail to a generator, they would have enough power to light all of Urbana for weeks on end.

One time, the boy came down with the flu and wasn't able to leave the house to go to school, much less to the ice cream parlor. Four days later, when he was well again, he took Gar out for their customary walk around town. The dog trotted happily beside him, no leash required, only stopping a few times to sniff at bushes and hydrants and trees. But when the pair came into view of Kerr's Sweet Shop, Gar suddenly left the boy's side and dashed across Main Street. Pausing on the far corner, he glanced back, as if imploring his owner to follow. So the boy did, following Gar right up through the door into the ice cream parlor.

The boy walked up to the counter, asked for "the usual," and sifted through the change in his pocket to pay. But instead of the usual ten cents—a nickel for each cone—the man working as ice cream scooper said the boy owed a quarter.

The boy was confused. He'd ordered only two single-scoop cones: one vanilla, one chocolate, just as he always did. That should be a dime.

The man behind the counter smiled and said, "Well, your dog there's been comin' in the past few afternoons around this time, and he kept barkin' and barkin' and wouldn't stop. We figured since you always get a vanilla cone for him, and he likes them so well, that we'd just give him some ice cream—even though you weren't here. So we've sorta been keepin' a tab for him. I hope that's okay."

The boy laughed and assured the man that it certainly was. In fact, he told them to keep the tab running if Gar came in by himself again—which the dog occasionally did over the course of his long, happy life.

Even many years later, long after his children had children of their own, my grandfather still got a kick out of telling the story about Gar, his crazy dog with his very own charge account at the local ice cream parlor.

Common Language and ESP
(Extra-Sensory Pups)

Call of the Wild

By D. Lynn Black

At first glance, Maya is your typical high-octane, lovin'-life boxer with a brain like a mousetrap and a nose for mischief. A natural clown, her favorite party trick is backing up to the couch and sitting down just like a person. I half expect her to ask for the TV remote.

But beyond the endearing, if sometimes incorrigible, personality lies an uncanny telepathic ability. She carries out commands before I voice them, and I swear, when our eyes meet she can read my mind and respond to my emotions. For years, my friends have teased me. "It's the Vulcan Mind Meld!" they'd say, dismissing this psychic interchange as mumbo jumbo. But even I never realized the startling scope of this rare communication—until the day it was put to a remarkable test.

It happened when Maya and I spent the summer in a remote wilderness area of northern Minnesota. We ventured out on daily hikes, which made our bond even stronger. One day Maya stopped in her tracks, hackles up, staring intently into a thicket. Through the bramble I made out a long, grayish muzzle and upright ears. A fox maybe? I cautiously moved closer until I was staring into the amber eyes of a wolf! It was the first one I'd seen in the wild. I knew attacks on humans were virtually unheard of, but if he got into a tussle with Maya she wouldn't stand a chance.

Fortunately, the wolf seemed as startled as we were and scampered away through the brush. After that, we spotted him regularly. He was a handsome silver dun with a dark patch over one eye. I decided to call him Pirate. I figured he was a lone wolf until one day I observed Pirate trekking along a bluff with his family, a pack of seven: his beautiful dove gray mate, their three gangly, teenaged pups, and two subordinate adults. Curious, they stopped to watch us. Maya, too, seemed intrigued, and I could only wonder if both sides recognized they were canine cousins.

Over the weeks we crossed paths often. The pack let us come within twenty-five feet, sensing a mutual respect, that we meant them no harm. In the evenings I could hear their choral howlings in the distance and found their melancholy night music oddly comforting. One morning Maya and I were hiking along a little-used dirt trail when the sound of motors broke the lazy silence. Three ATVs whizzed past. They peeled off around the bend and then returned, abruptly stopping in front of us—a trio of twenty-something male riders, rather scruffy around the edges. The burly copper-haired leader switched off his engine.

"Nice day for a walk, huh?" he greeted laconically.

Maya's low growl made me immediately uneasy. She didn't like the look of them, and neither did I.

"You live around here?" the beefy redhead asked.

"Yeah, a little ways back," I replied, in a breezy tone that belied my wariness.

I wanted to move on, but my feet felt strangely bolted to the ground. The men didn't seem to be in any hurry, which was further unsettling. Red lit up a cigarette, leaning against his ATV while the other two sat stoically on their vehicles.

"You all by yourself?" he asked. His intense gaze shot a chill through me.

"Oh, I'm never by myself," I replied, trying to smile confidently while looking down at Maya.

Red's buddies exchanged wry smirks.

Suddenly, Maya turned and shot off into the woods. My heart stopped. How could she abandon me at a time like this to go squirrel chasing! Fighting panic, I struggled to rein in my fear. *Stay cool*, I told myself. *Act like nothing's wrong.*

Long awkward moments crawled by in tense, agonizing silence, punctuated by Red's unnerving stares. Why didn't they move on?

"Of course, you're never alone for long on this trail," I ventured in a loud voice that didn't sound at all like mine. "Actually, the traffic out here really picks up about now."

"That's funny—we haven't seen anyone, have we boys?" the leader remarked, darting a bemused glance at his cronies.

I didn't like where this was going. Images popped into my head of unspeakable things that could happen to a woman alone in the woods.

Just then came a rustling behind me. To my great relief it was Maya, bounding through the trees to stand at my side. Incredibly, on her heels was the wolf pack, led by Pirate. Maya had summoned the cavalry!

I watched, awestruck, as the pack spread out in a semicircle behind me. Heads lowered, tails straight out, their piercing gold eyes aimed dead ahead on the ATVers. I couldn't believe what I was seeing, but there was no mistake. This was a threat formation, a grandstand show of intimidation, wolf-pack style!

The men froze in stunned silence, the look on their ashen faces priceless. Several intense minutes ticked by while the pack didn't budge an inch. Who would blink first? Finally, in almost comical slow motion, the petrified trio fired up their engines and then sped off, not to be seen again.

I collapsed in joyous relief to hug my canine heroine. For just an instant a look seemed to pass between Maya and Pirate. I swear I saw Pirate grin before he turned and bolted with his pack back into the wild. I had just witnessed something wholly extraordinary, seemingly beyond instinct, and clearly beyond mere chance. Maya's SOS call of the wild had bridged the worlds of human and animal, domestic and feral, while losing nothing in translation. I wondered if perhaps there were no boundaries after all, only a communication gap—born of ignorance, misunderstanding, and Homo sapiens arrogance.

As Maya has shown me, maybe we just needed to open the channels—and listen.

Hart of Gold

By Aubrey H. Fine, Ed.D.

I t's been over twenty-five years now since I began using animals in my child psychotherapy practice. A number of the
children I see feel painfully isolated and unlovable, and I've
found that something about the animals—whether dogs, birds,
fish, or rabbits—seems to reach through their often self-imposed
walls and allows them to give and receive love.

One of the most memorable of these children was a young
teenager I'll call Sarah. The thirteen-year-old was referred to me
when her school counselor observed that Sarah seemed deeply
demoralized and withdrawn.

At our first session, Sarah arrived wearing a baseball cap pulled
down so low on her head that the brim hid her eyes. She was
overweight, wore her hair in a chin-length bob, and was trembling—clearly she was very frightened. When I greeted her, she
barely responded; her voice was practically a whisper.

Then Hart, my black Labrador "co-therapist," walked quietly
to Sarah's side and sat close to her chair. Unlike my other dogs,
Hart never nudges anyone's hand to ask for attention; she gives
comfort simply by being nearby. At that first meeting, Hart sat by

Sarah, ready to be petted if Sarah felt like it. Sarah didn't react to Hart's appearance at first, but after a few seconds, she reached out and began stroking Hart's head. Within minutes, her trembling decreased. During our session, she spoke very little, and when she did speak, it was very quietly; at times she would shiver with fear. The only time she seemed to relax was when she touched Hart.

Sarah and I spent the first two sessions getting acquainted. Our progress was slow, as Sarah divulged little, but I didn't want to push her. My goal was to build a relationship with this obviously troubled girl—a connection based on trust. I did learn that Sarah had no real friends and that she felt like an outcast. She was afraid to speak up, afraid to approach others—she said she was pretty much "just afraid."

Our work together was interrupted after the second session. Sarah's fear and loneliness had been driving her to cut herself on her arm, initially with a pin and then with a razor blade. For months, she'd kept her wounds hidden from everyone, but eventually she showed her arm to a girl at school, who became frightened and told the counselor. The counselor immediately had Sarah placed in a psychiatric facility. Although this was terribly frightening for Sarah, it was necessary for her safety. It was also the turning point in our relationship.

During the almost two weeks she was in the facility, Sarah called periodically to let me know how she was doing. I was glad that the work Hart and I had done to earn her trust had succeeded, and she felt she could turn to me for support.

On Sarah's first visit with me after her release, she was still quiet but seemed more at ease. As we talked, Hart sat close by her chair, more alert than usual to Sarah's every move.

At one point in our session, Sarah's reserve finally crumbled. Pushing up her left sleeve, she showed me her newly healed scars. As she lowered her arm, we both noticed that Hart's eyes remained fixed on the crisscrossed, reddish-pink lines etched into her skin, the visible traces of her inner pain. As I watched, Hart lifted her gaze to meet Sarah's eyes with an expression that I can only describe as puzzled. For a long moment, the girl and the dog just looked at one another. Then Hart lowered her head and began softly and tenderly licking the scars on Sarah's arm. For a startled second, Sarah sat still, and then she bent over Hart and held her close.

Something shifted in Sarah that day. During that session, we talked about her cutting, and she was honest with me about it. From that point on, our progress accelerated.

Sarah's connection with Hart grew stronger as the weeks went by. Some afternoons, we took my dogs to a park near the office. I walked my other dog, PJ, while Sarah walked Hart. She would open up as we walked along, chatting together, the dogs trotting ahead of us on their leashes. On these walks, I often carried my umbrella cockatoo, Snowflake, on my shoulder, and Sarah got a real kick out of that.

At the park, I saw an entirely new side to Sarah: she giggled while she played with Hart—rubbing the dog's belly and scratching her head. When Hart got excited, she didn't just wag her tail; her whole back end would begin to wag, going from side to side at a mile a minute. The sight always made Sarah laugh out loud. It was so rewarding to see the unmistakable happiness in her eyes.

Over the next eight months, Sarah made many positive changes in her life—her academic performance improved dramatically, she began to volunteer at a nursery school, and she especially loved helping at the local animal shelter. Slowly, we began to see less of each other, until one afternoon we agreed her therapy was complete.

Two years after our last session, I received an e-mail from Sarah, telling me she was doing well and thanking me—and Hart—for our help during that difficult time in her life. Some months after that, she came to the office to visit. As we talked about her past, she recalled how she'd felt separated from others and empty inside.

"It was like a glass wall divided the world into two," she told me. "I was on the other side and couldn't get in. You and Hart helped me learn to break through that wall." She turned to look at Hart and smiled. "It's funny that it was a dog that taught me how to talk to other people."

My work with Sarah showed me, once again, the healing power of animals. At difficult moments, Sarah had held on to Hart, clasping the dog in her arms and burying her face in Hart's warm, soft fur. I believe it was the silent comfort of Hart's presence that enabled Sarah to finally verbalize what she needed and wanted to say.

Sarah was simply one of those children who healed best with the help of a security blanket—only in this case, the blanket came in the form of a black Labrador named Hart.

Somewhere Yonder

By Lisa Price

W e both know the end of our time together is approaching, my dog and I, but still we hold on. I lie on the floor, my arm around his furry neck, scratching his chest as I watch a marathon on TV. He's lived a long life for a shepherd-Lab mix, nearly fifteen years, but his black coat is still as glossy and thick as it was in his puppy days. People often ask if he is part wolf.

Watching the marathoners reminds me of all the miles Kliban and I have run through the years. We have probably run ten thousand miles together as I trained for races, through all seasons. I was there when Kliban was born, and I named him after a cartoonist I liked. His presence has been the one constant thread, the singular unchanging color, in the tapestry of the past fifteen years.

Threads of that tapestry have unraveled, people have gone, and there are memories that only the two of us share. "He's just a dog," people who have never had a dog might say. But there is a wisdom, born in the shared years, that glows in those luminous brown eyes, now clouded with the blue of old age above a graying muzzle.

When we hiked the Appalachian Trail together, we fell into a pattern that mirrored the way he always lived in my life, his self-appointed guardianship of me. He always trotted ahead to wait for me, standing protectively where he could scan the trail ahead while keeping me in sight. As I slept, he protected me, once even charging a wild boar that rooted around our tent in Tennessee. Twice on the trail he disobeyed me. Once, in Virginia, he returned from his vantage point and blocked my path. As I kept trying to go around him I grew irritated—until I finally heard the ominous shakes of the rattlesnake up ahead.

And in New York, where we had hiked a long two days without water during a drought, he suddenly disappeared for a stretch of many minutes. I yelled at him when he finally reappeared and approached, until he rubbed his wet chest against my legs and then led me to the water.

The words "good dog" made him quiver with happiness, and that was all he ever wanted.

But now the arthritic hips have finally failed, the vision has dimmed, and the internal systems have worn out. Still, how I dread that last good-bye, that scene at the veterinarian's office when he will be "put to sleep."

And yet, as I hold him and feel his thin shoulders, I know it is time. So I tell him so and start to cry. "Tomorrow," I tell him, "I'll make the appointment. You've been so tough and brave, protecting me all your life. It's okay."

"You're a good dog," I tell him, and he responds with a quiver. "It's me you've been waiting for, I finally understand. I love you, and I'll never forget you. I wish you could be with me my whole life, but I'm ready. It's okay. You can rest now."

I can't stand it. I get up and go into the other room, turn on the computer and try to work for a while. When I return twenty minutes later, Kliban has gone, with dignity and peace, protecting me this one last time.

He is wrapped in a quilt made of T-shirts from the running races he helped me train for and is buried in a shady spot with a view of the mountains. And he is somewhere yonder, on the long trail, where he has gone ahead to wait for me.

Saved

By Deborah Blair

My second son, Nick, was born on September 18, 1986; my first golden retriever, Rocky, just a few weeks later. It's hard to remember now which one was a funnier, more mischievous little troublemaker. Suffice it to say, I had both hands full—and then some—for the next couple of years.

I'm not sure why I thought bringing home a baby and a puppy at virtually the same time was the best way to do things, but I'd always wanted a golden retriever, and at the time it just seemed right. Luckily, Rocky loved both my boys from day one.

The four of us had great times together. My older son, Tony, was nearly three and walking on his own, so we'd often head off to the park, Tony holding my hand, baby Nick in the stroller, and Rocky's leash tied to the stroller's handle. When Rocky got bigger, his rambunctious ways sometimes led to tears and bruises, especially as little Nick was learning to walk, so Rocky had to stay home more during this stage. But he always adjusted willingly to whatever we needed.

One morning I was giving Tony a bath when my husband, Gary, stuck his head in the door.

"Where's Nick?" he asked.

I stared at him blankly. "I thought he was with you."

A look of concern passed between us, and off Gary ran to find Nick, who was about thirteen months old at the time. After a couple of minutes, Gary's strained face appeared at the doorway again.

"I can't find him."

Unless your child has been lost, you can't know the wretched sickness that grips you at these words. My heart started to pound. "Is the front door closed?" I asked.

I grabbed Tony out of the tub, and we ran to the front door. It was a warm June day in Los Angeles—the front door was open; the screen door was closed, but unlatched. Shaken, I rattled off locations to check: "Backyard?" "Garage?" "Our bedroom?"

Gary took off for the next-door neighbor's house, while I set Tony down in his room and frantically began looking under beds, in cabinets, and in every nook and cranny of the backyard. I met Gary at the screen door, and his face told me the story: my baby was gone.

Seized with horror, I thought, *He's been kidnapped!* Even in our friendly, family-oriented neighborhood, I suddenly felt there could be bad guys around any corner.

In a blind panic, I ran to the front yard and began screaming Nick's name. Neighbors came out of their houses to see why the normally quiet mother of two was having a nervous breakdown out in her yard. I ran down the street and around the corner, desperate to see his sturdy little form. No Nick. Meanwhile, Gary told the rest of the neighbors that Nick was missing, and they ran to look for him, some heading to their cars, one running to our house to watch Tony.

I sped back to the house. Seeing me return empty-handed, Gary yelled that he was calling the police and ran inside. I jogged to the opposite corner, still hollering Nick's name. I was crying, hysterical, in shock. People tried to talk to me, but I wouldn't listen. I pushed past them, calling Nick's name, again and again. One neighbor tried to get me to come inside, but I couldn't hear what she was saying over the noise of my crying. *My babe . . . my Nick.* Running back down the street to the first corner, I rounded it and continued to run.

Then, I saw them. It was the most beautiful sight I have ever seen in my life: my curly-headed baby boy, in his little blue pants and striped shirt, toddling down the street in my direction, Rocky by his side. Nick had one hand on Rocky's broad golden back and was using the dog to steady himself as he tottered along, smiling happily and talking to Rocky in a baby-talk gibberish. Trailing about ten feet behind the two of them was an elderly lady with a quizzical look on her face.

With a huge cry, I ran across the street and swept Nick up into my arms. Rocky began jumping around happily, and the lady came up to us, saying, "Oh, my, was he lost? I've been following them because it just didn't look right for a young baby to be taking a dog for a walk."

Nick looked totally confused as I sobbed and kissed him. Neighbors came running, and happy faces surrounded me, but all I wanted to do was get Nick safely back home. I carried him down the street to our house. Gary met me at the gate, and we went

inside. As I sat down on the couch, holding Nick tightly, still sobbing and kissing him, Rocky came in somberly and lay down, resting his big head on my feet.

Some may scoff, but let them think what they will. I believe
that when Nick toddled out that door, Rocky knew it wasn't right.
He went with him to keep him safe, his friend and protector. That
big, goofy puppy turned out to be my baby's guardian angel.

Rocky lived to be a little over thirteen, always a cherished member of our family. He may not have been a champion, or even very
obedient or good at tricks, but he was so much more to us than
that. He saved us all when he gently guided baby Nick home.

Rocky instilled in me a deep love for dogs in general and
golden retrievers in particular that has never changed. Because
of him, I now breed, train, and show golden retrievers—always
conscious of the miracle they are in our lives. It's my way of trying to repay Rocky's amazing gift.

READER/CUSTOMER CARE SURVEY

We care about your opinions! Please take a moment to fill out our online Reader Survey at **http://survey.hcibooks.com**.

As a **"THANK YOU"** you will receive a **VALUABLE INSTANT COUPON** towards future book purchases

as well as a **SPECIAL GIFT** available only online! Or, you may mail this card back to us.

(PLEASE PRINT IN ALL CAPS)

First Name	MI.	Last Name

Address		City

State	Zip	Email

---

1. Gender
☐ Female ☐ Male

2. Age
☐ 8 or younger
☐ 9-12   ☐ 13-16
☐ 17-20 ☐ 21-30
☐ 31+

3. Did you receive this book as a gift?
☐ Yes   ☐ No

4. Annual Household Income
☐ under $25,000
☐ $25,000 - $34,999
☐ $35,000 - $49,999
☐ $50,000 - $74,999
☐ over $75,000

5. What are the ages of the children living in your house?
☐ 0 - 14   ☐ 15+

6. Marital Status
☐ Single
☐ Married
☐ Divorced
☐ Widowed

7. How did you find out about the book?
(please choose one)
☐ Recommendation
☐ Store Display
☐ Online
☐ Catalog/Mailing
☐ Interview/Review

8. Where do you usually buy books?
(please choose one)
☐ Bookstore
☐ Online
☐ Book Club/Mail Order
☐ Price Club (Sam's Club, Costco's, etc.)
☐ Retail Store (Target, Wal-Mart, etc.)

9. What attracts you most to a book?
(please choose one)
☐ Title
☐ Cover Design
☐ Author
☐ Content

10. What subject do you enjoy reading about the most?
(please choose one)
☐ Parenting/Family
☐ Relationships
☐ Recovery/Addictions
☐ Health/Nutrition
☐ Christianity
☐ Spirituality/Inspiration
☐ Business Self-help
☐ Women's Issues
☐ Sports
☐ Pets

FOLD HERE

The ULTIMATE Series

Comments

A golden enjoying a
first autumn romp.

Aspen, a visually impaired and deaf Great Dane, learned over thirty hand signals to communicate with his mom.

What are you waiting for? Can't you read the sign? Adopt me!

What am I thinking?
Let me spell it out:
W-A-L-K.

There's nothing better
than a well-timed kiss.

Whatever it was, I
didn't do it, and if I
did, I didn't mean it.

The sport of canine agility is open to all breeds and mixes, and is a great way to bond with your dog.

This Australian cattle dog is just begging for a swimming partner.

A Leg to Stand On

By Pierre O'Rourke

Okay, so everyone thinks *their* dog is so special. Is it my fault I happen to know mine actually is? My Australian cattle dog–border collie mix, Nubble, is a peaceful soul. He loves all beings, no matter how many legs they have. Except birds. He finds our feathered friends *foul*—but as you'll see, he has his reasons.

One day, when Nubble and I were walking in downtown Scottsdale, we passed in front of City Hall where there's a cement pond with an assortment of birdies in residence, including two black swans. One of the swans decided it wise to charge out of the water and nip at Nubble, who after a few warning growls, finally took action by soft-mouthing the feathered treasure by the neck and leading her back to the water. Undeterred, Madam Swan repeated this unsettling approach to my dog a few weeks later. Again, Nubble dutifully escorted her back into the pond. The third time that we walked past, she wisely opted to leave Nubble alone.

But sometimes it's Nubble who won't leave the birds alone. Nubble and I run together, often past the golf courses of Scottsdale, where if the chance presents itself, he will make time to ride herd on the ducks waddling around on shore. He'll corral and march them into the water, where he continues to herd them into a tight formation as he dog-paddles around the quacking critters. After a few laps and loops, he dives beneath them, then suddenly surfaces in the center of the group to a bedlam of quacking and barking as the ducks take flight. Oh, for a video camera to catch the moment "as dog gooses ducks."

Nubble also feels it's his duty to keep the patio of our favorite coffee shop bird-free. Starbucks, aka Starbarks, has known Nubble since I adopted him from the Arizona Humane Society when he was two months old. I'd studied the books by the Monks of New Skete and decided to follow their dog-socializing suggestion to expose a dog, no matter what age, to fifty people within the first thirty days of bringing him home. As a result, Nubble has come to view the shop as a spot where bipeds come to pet canines, getting their coffee as an afterthought. The one we frequent at the mall now keeps a couple of dog dishes of fresh water out on their patio.

The Scottsdale Fashion Square Mall, in its infinite wisdom, installed sharp spikes around all the recessed lighting to keep the birds away. Unfortunately, the birds—the pigeons in particular— have found that the spikes make a dandy support for their nests, and have made themselves right at home. However, they haven't fared as well with the water dishes when Nubble is on paw.

Nubble is not prejudiced. Wrens, sparrows, or pigeons—none are deemed worthy of the patio crumbs or the water in "his" water dish. He chases them all away with a loud bark if they dare to trespass.

One morning as I sat out on the patio sipping coffee, with Nubble resting quietly near my chair, a pigeon, soft gray with a smattering of white about the chest and neck, alit a couple of feet from the sacred water dish.

Nubble stood up and turned his head one way; the pigeon turned her head to the other. They reverse-mirrored each other like that a few times as I quickly set my cup down to avoid throwing it in the air when my dog let loose his inevitable warning bark. As their gazing continued, I spied the bird's single leg. Nubble seemed to have observed sooner than I that the pigeon had only one leg to stand on.

The pigeon took a hop closer; Nubble sat down. Another hop. Nubble lay down with his head a short distance from the bowl's lip. The next hop brought the bird just inches from the bowl. To my amazement, Nubble's shoulders relaxed. The daring bird then hopped atop the rim of his dish; Nubble smiled. (Don't kid yourself—dogs do smile.) A shopper stood transfixed as her eyes welled with tears. "My God," she said. "He knows."

The bird dipped its charcoal beak to drink, gave a soft coo-sound as it stood upright, then dipped its head two more times. Other birds landed a few feet away, but Nubble's mere glance was enough for them to take flight. The pigeon took one more gulp, then craned its head as if to make sure the cool water thoroughly lubricated its throat. Thirst quenched, it hopped down, pogo-sticked right past Nubble's watchful eye, and flew away. At that moment, one of the other birds returned. Nubble immediately leapt to attention, barking the alarm, and I finally managed to spill my drink.

We've seen that pigeon a few times since then. The dance and communication always remain the same: a piece of performance art I call "Trust and Compassion in Action." We've named his one-legged friend Eileen.

The Greeting

By Sheri Ryan

For over a decade I took it for granted, but sometimes it's the little everyday things that you miss the most when they're gone. I'm talking about "the greeting."

For all those years, every time I came home, whether at the end of the day or from church or from a quick trip to the store down the street, my dog, Zosia, never failed to give me a hero's welcome. Somehow, she was able hear my van from several houses away and, by family accounts, at the first sound would leave her favorite spot upstairs and come barreling down the steps, often knocking down anything or anyone who got in her way. She would position herself at the window by the door and push back the curtain with her nose. Then she would stand there with her entire body wagging in joyful anticipation of my entrance into the house.

As I approached the door, I could see her eager, smiling face at the window, letting me know that she had waited all day long (or just fifteen minutes) for my return. As I stepped through the doorway, she would rear up on her hind legs and nearly knock me over with her front paws as she slathered me with leaping kisses.

Considering that Zosia is a ninety-pound Rottweiler-shepherd mix, I always found it best to sit down on the chair by the door as soon as possible, so as not to topple over backward and end up sprawled on the floor, completely at the mercy of her loving assault. In between kisses, she would cry and howl as if to ask, *Why did you leave me, and what took you so long?*

When she was done with the kissing, she would thump her hind end against me so that I could commence with the petting. When she'd had her fill of that, she would throw herself onto the floor for her routine belly rub, and after that, we'd top off the whole event with a cookie. She would then hang out with me while I made dinner or did whatever chores needed to be done, until she felt comfortable that I wasn't going anywhere, at which point she would make her way upstairs to lie down in her spot once again.

Zosia is twelve years old now and has had a couple of serious accidents that have left her poor body weak and frail. She now spends most of her day confined to her favorite room. Needless to say, my daily homecomings are vastly different than in the past. At first, completely caught up in the busyness of my daily life, I couldn't figure out why, shortly after my arrival, she would launch into loud and demanding barking from upstairs that just would not cease. And then it hit me—it was "the greeting." She hadn't forgotten, but I had.

Her whole life, Zosia has lavished on me something that no human being has: unconditional love. Regardless of how I look or what awful things I say or do, she simply loves me and longs to be with me every day, without fail. Now, in her golden years, it is I who have failed her. But as always, my furry child forgives me.

When I come home now, she gives me a good thirty seconds to put my things down and hang up my coat before she starts to call out to me. I reassure her that I am on my way as I climb the stairs. Her sweet face, now gray with age, peeks out from behind the chair that keeps her safely confined while I am away. I see her, and I smile. Her whole body wags with joyful anticipation of my coming into the room. Her legs shake from trying to support her body. I lovingly caress her and receive her gentle kisses.

For as long as God allows me, I will lavish on her the same love she has faithfully given to me all of these years, and I will never again forget "the greeting."

Langley

By Calder Reid

Langley, my chocolate Labrador retriever mix, was a good employee. The trust he won from the public always enhanced his end-of-season evaluations. I'd write, "Highly recommended for rehire. Langley engages with the public effortlessly. In addition, he works well with others and is a self-starter." For all these accolades, he didn't have to do much: he just had to be himself.

Not that our job with the USDA Forest Service in California's John Muir Wilderness didn't have its challenges. Along with hiking two thousand feet in elevation on any given day, we were tasked with speaking to every member of the public we came in contact with. Wilderness permits, secured through a lottery system, were required on this popular trail, and with this privilege came responsibilities. It was my job to check permits and rattle off the ethics and regulations for the area. Not everyone is receptive to this kind of presence in "their" wilderness, but fortunately for me, most were receptive to the charms of Langley.

The Mt. Whitney Trail, our main territory, was busy every day during the snow-free season. Early mornings produced hundreds of people determined to complete the long trail in one day. Though they were racing against daylight, the hikers looked like slow-moving ants as they climbed toward our spot, a switchback on a high ridge. Langley would sit in the soft pine needles, and I'd sit on a large flat boulder with my backpack and radio.

Knowing we were sure to maximize public contacts by staying in one place, we would get there early and wait, watching the sunrise creep up and over the Sierra granite to warm my fingers and toes and Langley's dark chocolate coat.

By 6:00 AM, the first waves of hikers would arrive at our switchback, nicknamed by another ranger, "Bust You Point," to find me, the lone female Mt. Whitney Wilderness Ranger in a drab olive-green uniform checking wilderness permits—hardly what anybody wants to see on their trek to the top of the highest mountain in the contiguous United States. My unofficial backup was Langley. Though he had a sweet disposition, he wasn't a small dog and he was certainly capable of defending his pack. Seeing Langley, the public knew there were boundaries they could not cross.

Over time I learned to pay attention to his reactions to people. He could sense a negative person thirty feet away, producing a low growl that only I could hear. My official backup was a government-issued radio, a booklet of citations, and verbal judo learned at a four-day law enforcement course for handling pumped-up, privileged attitudes. The real firepower was with the "local" police department, four miles and a thousand feet down-trail, ten miles by car. Any response from them to a bad situation would be too late; we were on our own.

Fortunately, with Langley at my side, the majority of our contacts with the public went without a hitch. As soon as approaching hikers saw this friendly Labrador, they knew at least one of us
would be forgiving. Some were standoffish, but their reservations
didn't last long. Langley could work anybody. He'd bat his droopy
eyes and move to the end of his leash to improve his chances at
winning their affection. People, pleased to connect with a canine,
responded with a simple pat on Langley's head or perhaps a hearty
scratch on the rump.

The questions and comments were fired off immediately: "Oh,
look, how sweet! What's his name? What breed is he? Where did
you get him? I miss my dog back at home." Langley took it in like
a sponge; he knew he was the object of all the fuss. Faces were
offered and Langley kissed them. When an affectionate hiker
started to leave, Langley would lift one front paw and strike it in
the air, a last ditch effort at retaining his admirer's attention. "Oh,
he's so cute; look! Sorry, puppy, I have to go."

One benefit of the inquiries about Langley was that they broke
the ice and postponed the official nature of my presence. Between
"Good morning" and "Where are you headed?" my scripted opening lines, Langley made it evident that I was a friendly ranger.
After all the small talk came my delivery of the line that paid the
hourly wage and provided for Langley's training treats: "May I see
your wilderness permit?" Langley didn't care about the paperwork;
he waited patiently until he could greet the next visitor or get
back to traipsing around the woods with me.

I don't think he could ever have imagined such a wonderful
life when he was waiting on death row in the County Animal

Shelter. The day I adopted him, he was lying in a plastic bed in the back of his run, chin propped up, looking intently at me. All the other potential adoptees were barking and begging to be considered. Langley's demeanor intrigued me, and I asked the attendant if I could take him outside. As soon as we were in the grassy enclosed area, I let him off his leash, and he ran around with delight, leapt over the small creek, and began to mark territory. *This dog enjoys being outside*, I said to myself. *Perfect!*

I adopted him that day and named him after the 14,027-foot peak in the southern Sierra Nevada range near Mt. Whitney. I took him to an obedience class, and we worked daily on mastering the commands. Langley was a fast learner. Not only was he smart, but he also seemed genuinely proud to bond with me.

One day the instructor asked Langley and me to go out in front of the class and "show everyone how it's supposed to look." I said, "Langley, heel!" and when I took off, he took off; when I stopped, he sat. But it didn't end there. He craned his neck to look up at me with an adoring look in his eyes. It was as if he were saying, "Is there anything else you want me to do?" One of the students piped up and said, "That's not fair. He's crazy about her!" Soon, Langley and I were spending so much time together that communication didn't require commands; hand signals were enough.

After hiking long stretches on the trail, Langley and I would choose a small piece of ground to call home for the night. With his keener set of eyes and ears, he became the armor I relaxed behind as I settled into camp and slipped into my bag to sleep. Langley alerted me to anything that required attention, such as hikers lost off-trail or black bears searching for human food. And although there was only a soft and cuddly Labrador in our tent, passersby—whether two- or four-footed—heard what sounded like the deep bark of a Rottweiler.

Tucked into my bag one night, I heard a bear approach suddenly, paws crunching in the gravelly ground close by. Langley and I both sat up in the tent and listened. Langley let out a low, quiet growl. My heart pounding loudly, I asked Langley, "What's that?" which was code for "Go for it!" He immediately lurched forward and let out a single bark that turned into ten as it echoed off the granite walls rising up from the lake below. I jumped, but probably not as quickly as that bear. Our wild friend didn't return, and Langley and I slept soundly through the rest of the night. That kind of protection was priceless. I didn't need a gun or even a pile of rocks in front of my tent to throw at a visiting bear. I had Langley. Who knows how many potentially bad situations he dissipated by his mere presence?

Langley and I patrolled together for eleven years. Not many people remembered me from year to year, but they remembered Langley. I can't count how many times I heard, "You were here last year. I remember your brown dog. Langley, right?"

Eventually though, the work and elevation became too much for Langley's aging body. I cried the first time I had to leave him with a trusted friend and drive off toward the trailhead without him. The sound of a zipper always made his ears perk up, so that morning I packed my backpack when he wasn't around to hear. He knew that something had changed that day, but he never held it against me.

Later, in the sad days and nights after he died, I looked at photo after photo of Langley and me captured in time in stunningly beautiful places: on the tops of Sierra passes, beside green meadows and crystal-clear blue lakes, beneath the open, expansive sky. His trail had been long and full of joy and purpose; more than any dog could wish for. That special shelter dog touched not only my heart but also the hearts of many others. Though we'd come to a lot of trail junctions in our travels, this was the one where we had to go our separate ways.

I'm grateful Langley carried me to this fork in the road. It would have been a much more difficult and lonely journey were it not for him. I know our trails will meet again; junctions just mark different ways of getting to the same place.

Teachers
and Healers

Love Springs Eternal

By Ailene Wilson as told to Amanda Borozinski

I t was a crisp April morning, perfect for planting. I set the tray of dahlia bulbs down next to me in the sun-warmed grass and imagined how the straight row would look in full bloom. "Beautiful," I said to myself, beginning to dig a small hole. I couldn't wait to get all the bulbs in the ground, sprinkle them with water, and then let nature take over. Covering the last bulb, I glanced over my shoulder, expecting to see the neat, freshly tamped mounds. What I saw instead brought a scream to my lips.

"Annie! No!"

While planting the bulbs, I had, for the first time in weeks, forgotten about Annie. Now I could see what had kept her so quiet. Every time I had planted a bulb, she had dug it up. Nine slightly chewed and very moist bulbs now sat in the dirt next to nine empty holes.

She cocked her head to one side as I said, "Bad dog!"

I gathered up my bulbs and wondered (for the hundredth time) what had possessed me to say "Yes" to another dog. At seventy-three, I wanted to travel and garden, not clean up after a puppy.

Prior to Annie, our "Golden Years" had been going along just as I planned—three beautiful grandchildren, savings in the bank, and our health.

Then Gordon had started talking about getting a dog.

"Puppies are so cute," he said over his morning oatmeal.

"They're so much company," he added during our nightly cribbage game.

"They give so much love," he reminded me right before church.

Every time he mentioned getting a dog, I said the same thing, "No more dogs!"

I didn't see the pink tongues and fat bellies he did. I saw reality—dog hair everywhere, walks on cold mornings, potty-training mishaps, and chewed shoes. We'd had a dog nearly every year of our marriage. Wasn't that enough?

A few months before our fifty-first wedding anniversary, a friend just happened to come by for a visit with her two Australian shepherds. I knew Gordon was up to something.

The morning of our anniversary, I woke up first and made breakfast. After finishing his coffee, Gordon announced that he had made reservations for us at a nice restaurant, but first we were going to "just look" at some puppies. "I heard about a couple with a brand new litter of Australian shepherd pups. Let's just take a look."

Not exactly a trip to Alaska, I thought with a sigh.

We arrived in Oregon City around noon. The puppies had just finished a meal and were rolling around in the grass. With their roly-poly faces and open mouths, they seemed to be laughing. Gordon picked up the smallest puppy. She had blue eyes and a white and gray coat. "We could call her Annie," he said, handing the wriggling bundle to me.

I knew when I was beaten.

Eight weeks later, Annie was ours.

All of my misgivings about getting a dog proved right. Gordon called Annie "our little Tasmanian devil."

She chewed the heel off one of my shoes. She barked at anyone who came to the door. She jumped up on our friends and nearly pulled me to the ground every time I tried to take her for a walk.

Now she'd destroyed my bulbs, and I'd had it.

"Let's find a new home for her. She's too much for us," I said, depositing the bulbs in Gordon's lap.

Annie wagged her stump of a tail and looked up at us.

Gordon smiled. "She'll come around. You'll see. The two of you will be friends."

I didn't see a friend, but I could tell Gordon really loved her. Accepting that she was going to be staying, I sighed.

"All right," I said, "but she can't be outside when I garden anymore."

We didn't talk about getting rid of Annie again.

Then, two years later, the worst thing imaginable happened: Gordon got sick. I knew things were very wrong when I came home from church and found him lying in the dark bedroom. Annie, who was never allowed on the furniture, was stretched out beside him, her chin on his stomach.

This went on for three days. Finally, Gordon agreed to go to the emergency room.

Gordon was diagnosed with pancreatic cancer on a Monday. He passed away the following Friday.

When I came home from the hospital, Annie greeted me by resting her paw on my lap. I stroked her ears as I cried.

The first week after Gordon's death, I'd lie in bed and wonder, "Why should I get up? No one really needs me anymore."

Then I would feel a wet tongue licking my hand.

Annie wanted to go out.

I spent hours sitting in Gordon's favorite chair. Sometimes it was 6:00 PM before I noticed Annie whining in the kitchen. What does she want? Annie would look up at me and then stop pacing to look over at her food bowl. Oh, right! I forgot to feed her. Come to think of it, I hadn't eaten all day either. So many nights, those first few weeks, it was Annie inviting me to eat with her.

It was hard to get used to living alone after being married for nearly fifty-three years. I missed having someone in the house to talk to. One day I read a joke in the newspaper and laughed out loud. The sound of my laughter caught me off guard. I looked around. Annie looked up at me. So, I told her the joke. It almost seemed as though she got it.

This began a pattern: I would tell Annie about my day, we'd eat together, then I'd watch TV with her curled up at my feet.

I knew Annie loved Milk Bones and cooked carrots, so whenever I went to the grocery store I'd stock up. I noticed the drive-through bank tellers had dog treats in their window and started taking Annie with me to do my banking. Then I started taking Annie everywhere. On cool days she even waited for me in the car while I was at church.

One day in June, I was at the park throwing the Frisbee for Annie when a woman introduced herself and her border collie,

Shadow. Annie and Shadow hit it off immediately, so we began scheduling doggy playdates.

As the years passed, April, the month Gordon died, remained a very difficult time of year for me. One April morning, a few years after his death, I decided I wanted to plant something special to remind me of him.

"Let's go to the garden center," I said, grabbing my keys.

While Annie waited for me in the car, I walked down the rows of plants carefully reading the names. Roses. Daffodils. Geraniums. Dahlias!

Back home, I put on my gardening slacks and gloves. Annie settled in her bed, knowing gardening wasn't something we did together. But now I wanted her with me.

"Come on, Annie."

I opened the back door and we stepped out into the sunlight— together.

Happy Together

By Peggy Frezon

Anyone in their right mind wouldn't have given the little stray a second glance. He was bone-thin, each rib clearly visible beneath dirty brown fur. His head hung so low his nose scraped the ground. With his hunched spine and his tail tucked between his legs, he was shaped more like a bagel than a beagle mix.

He stood whimpering on our front steps. I knelt down and threw my arms around his scrawny neck. "He's perfect. Can we keep him?" I asked with six-year-old innocence. He winced at my touch. Still, I detected an almost imperceptible wag at the tip of his thick brown tail. "He's happy to be here," I decided. So, naturally, his name became Happy.

From the moment he came to live with us, Happy and I were inseparable. He followed me around the house. He lay at the foot of my bed at night. I took care of him, setting down hearty bowls of food until he filled out with a thick, barrel chest that revealed black Lab in his heritage.

Happy startled at loud noises and shrank away from men. My mom concluded that he'd been abused, then abandoned. As years passed, however, he never once growled or snapped or disobeyed. And the way he stuck to my side made me feel he was somehow grateful to me for rescuing him.

But as much as Happy needed me, I needed him, too. My family was changing, and I was hurt and confused. One day when I was in fifth grade, my mother came into my bedroom and put an arm gently around my shoulder. "I have something important to tell you," she said. "Dad and I are getting a divorce." I nodded, pretending to understand. But I didn't. After she left, I curled up on the floor beside Happy. He licked the salty tears off my cheeks, and I cried until I fell asleep.

That summer I spent my days at a camp in the Vermont mountains where my mother worked as camp nurse. My father stayed at his new home. Of course, Happy came with me.

Happy and I enjoyed every moment together at the camp. When I walked down the dirt path to the lake, Happy followed. As I splashed in the water, he waded in the shallow parts, poking his head in the cool wetness, trying to catch minnows. When I went into the arts and crafts building, he sat on the step outside the door until I came out again. Nothing could make him leave. It didn't matter if someone called him or tried to chase him or tempted him with food. Not even a thunderstorm, with the loud noises he feared so much, drove him away. He wouldn't budge a muscle until I was ready for him to accompany me back to my cabin.

After a rain, we'd play outside, splashing in the puddles together. He almost seemed to be dancing, up on his hind legs, jumping at the water I kicked up with my bare feet. He'd look at me with his deep brown eyes like he was trying to tell me something. I thought I knew what it was: he would always be there for me. I felt the same way, too.

I didn't see my father all summer, except one Saturday afternoon when he appeared at the camp. "Why is he here?" I wondered aloud as Happy and I wandered across the green field to where Dad had parked his car. He walked into the nurse's cabin to talk to Mom. I heard bits of the conversation as I approached.

". . . broken into . . . house next door . . . not safe . . . take the dog."

I burst through the cabin's screen door. "No!" I shouted. "No, you can't take Happy!"

"But honey," Mom tried to explain, "your father needs him. He could bark and scare away intruders."

"It wouldn't be forever. . . ." Dad started.

"No! You can't! You can't!" I spun around, pushing the screen door and letting it slam behind me.

When I got back outside, Happy wasn't there waiting for me. Where could he be, when I needed him so much? He was always able to comfort me when I was upset. But now, he was nowhere to be found.

I looked behind the dining hall and down by the rec center. No Happy. I searched down by the lake. Without my constant companion, I felt more alone than ever. I walked the nature path, calling for Happy, hoping to hear his husky woof, or the jingle of his tags on his collar. Nothing. Collapsing onto a stump by the path, I closed my eyes and sobbed. *God, please bring Happy back. I need him so.*

After I'd been in the woods for quite a while, I knew my mom would be getting worried. I figured it must be close to dinnertime. I walked down the path, alone and terribly troubled. When I reached the parking area beside the nurse's cabin, Mom and Dad were outside talking. I eyed Dad's old blue sedan. My heart sank. Could it be he had found Happy, and my dog was already in the car, about to be taken away from me?

What would I do without Happy? I'd be so lonely. And what about Happy? He'd never been away from me before, either. Besides, he was afraid of men. How would he get along alone with my dad?

I trudged to the car. Dad crossed his arms. "I don't think I can wait any longer," he said. "I've got to get ready for work tomorrow."

I peered in the car's tinted windows. Happy wasn't there!

Mom sighed. "I don't understand. He always comes when called." She turned to me. "Peggy, you try."

"Haaaaaapyyyy!" I called weakly, wishing with all my might that this time, just this once, he wouldn't come. "Happy, come here, boy!"

Nothing.

"Well," Dad sighed, opening the car door handle. "I guess that's that." He climbed into the driver's seat, closed the door, and pulled away. Mom and I just stood there as the late afternoon sun cast long shadows around us.

The car wheels kicked up great clouds of dust on the gravel driveway. As the dust was just settling, I heard a familiar jingle, and Happy came trotting around the corner. He sat right in front of me and looked into my eyes, almost smiling. I watched my dad's car disappear around the bend.

Mom glanced at me, raising an eyebrow, as if I'd had something to do with it. Of course, I hadn't. But how had Happy known? I reached down, scratched his ears, and smiled. I never could understand it. I just was certain Happy knew he was supposed to be with me.

Nothing more was said. Mom simply shook her head. I shrugged lightly, turned away, and skipped off down the path.

Happy was right at my heels.

 # Missy

By J. Vincent Dugas

It was a typical New England summer morning. The world was overcast with morning fog, and all was damp with dew. The ocean licked gently at the granite rock beach as the new day took its first, fresh breaths.

I seldom walked down to the beach this early. As I sat on my favorite boulder at the top of the rocky beach, I delighted in the company of my best lady friend, the ocean. For seventy years I had been close to her. I don't think I ever approached her without wishing her a "good morning" or offering a simple "hello." I know that she tossed me ashore countless times when I should have drowned, and she held my sailboat tall and safe in storms and wailing seas. In return, I have cherished a lifelong respect for her.

When I was a little boy, the oceanfront was always a place to play, to swim, and to search for things that had washed ashore from other places. I loved to walk the beach with an old pillowcase over my shoulder and scour the sand and rock crevasses for things not common to the waterfront. My mom called me a beachcomber, and my dad called me a scavenger, but every day, after I had spread out my pickings on the porch deck, they would

Some dogs love to comb the beach.

Wet kisses in the ear?
It's just life with a dog.

Dogs don't need to "talk" to make their feelings known. Their eyes tell it all.

Dogs seem to get a kick out of being dressed up, if we don't take it too far.

These dogs know two heads are better than one.

The weather is "snow problem" to this dog who lives for cold weather.

There's something so endearing about the mug of a pug.

Little dogs claim a big part of dog lovers' hearts.

join me in browsing through the little pieces of someone else's life. It was fun. At times, it was magical.

This morning, as I sat on my rock, still searching the beach for that out-of-place treasure, an odd object in the water caught my eye. Something was bobbing in the shallow lip of the water. It looked like an old rug or sheepskin, something that should not be in the water. My scavenger eyes tried to bring the object into focus, but my age demanded a closer squint. I picked my way down through rocks till I finally stumbled onto the beach itself. My heart dropped when I recognized what I had found. It was an animal, floating in the shallow water. I stepped closer and bent down to pull off the seaweed and other flotsam. It was a dog. *Oh, God!* I cried to myself. *Why?*

I stepped into the water and lifted her onto the beach. She had been tied with wire to some thin wooden slats, perhaps snow fencing. I knew she was dead, but still, I gently unwound most of the tangled wire. I pushed on her chest a few times after noticing water gurgling from her mouth. I held her up by her hind legs and squeezed her body between my knees. She looked like she'd been dead for some time, but I had to try. I covered her nose with my mouth and blew some air into her lungs, hoping for the impossible. What had happened to this poor soul?

Sadly, knowing it was in vain, I worked on the little animal for a while, and then, leaving her on the dune grass to dry in the sun, I walked up to the garage for a pair of cutting pliers to remove the remaining wire.

John, the gentleman who lived with his wife in the apartment over the garage and was more a house sitter than a houseman,

came back to the beach with me. We cut loose the remaining bits
of wire, both agreeing that it had surely been wound around the
dog by the hand of man. It was our consensus that she'd been tied
with the wire and tossed overboard, possibly to be used as shark
bait by some rogue fisherman. We shuddered at the lingering evidence of such evil.

I took the bottle of spring water John had brought and trick-
led a little into the dead dog's mouth to wash away the sand and
saltwater. A flicker of motion suddenly startled me.

"My God! Her tongue moved," I yelled.

John disagreed. It must've been a muscle or nerve that jumped,
he thought. I worked her chest a few more times and blew again
into her nose and mouth. Suddenly, a gush of water shot out of
her mouth, with a flutter of air behind it. Seconds passed and
then—as if God himself had blown air into her lungs—she sucked
in, coughed, and started to breathe in short, unsteady breaths.

John and I looked at each other in disbelief. She's alive! The
drowned dog is alive! We two old men ran her up to the house
and into a bathroom shower. I stood in the shower and held her
under the warm water to heat up her cold flesh. Then we dried her
with an electric hair dryer and wrapped her in a wool blanket and
an electric blanket and dropped oil in her eyes and honey water on
her tongue. She was breathing but had not yet come to.

I called my old friend Ralph, the local vet, and was told to keep
her warm for a while before bringing her to his clinic.

I can see her now, wrapped up in the huge comforter on my
bed. She was beautiful. At first I thought she was an Irish setter,
but she was too blond for that. She was mostly golden retriever we

thought, or perhaps, a little of each. She was breathing more steadily now, with no gurgling. Now, if she would just awaken . . . but we knew she could be brain damaged or otherwise badly injured. She could die at any time.

Nevertheless, at least she would not die alone, cold, wet, and afraid. Right now, she was the major attraction in a king-size bed in the master bedroom of a great home on the shores of New England, surrounded by concerned friends. This little girl was in kinder hands now. I ran my hand under the covers to feel her body. She was warming, and I could feel her heartbeat. If her brain hadn't been damaged, she might make it.

The doorbell rang, and much to our surprise we found the vet and one of his assistants, bearing a small bottle of oxygen and all sorts of equipment.

"We thought it better that the dog not be moved, so we brought the mountain to Mohammed."

Ralph had taken care of several of my pets throughout their lives. He examined the dog from head to tail, gave her a couple of shots, and attached a small nasal jet to feed her some oxygen and an intravenous drip for some liquids. He didn't know if she'd ever awaken, but he thought she had a good chance.

As the hours ticked by, our little group became larger with the addition of my wife and John's and, later, the return of Ralph. We all took turns sitting with the dog, massaging her paws and legs and stroking her sleeping face. During his shift John held her in his arms, singing to her and stroking her head as tears ran down his craggy face. Having witnessed the cruelty she had suffered, I guess John and I had suffered along with her.

That night my wife slept in a guest room, and I stayed in our bedroom with my adopted charge. I stretched out next to her and held her back against my own body, as I might hold a child. I drifted off, thinking that I'd give God a rest from all my prayers.

The sound was weird. I hadn't heard a sound like that since Shannon, my old Irish setter, sang in her sleep. It wasn't a snore. It was more a sighing kind of song. Here it was again, yet my setter had died many years ago. I awoke abruptly. My eyes snapped wide open, and I was up on my elbow. That song. It was here. I had not dreamed it. I listened again. The song was coming from her. The nearly dead animal next to me was singing on each exhaled breath. I patted her and looked at her face. Her eyes were partially opened. I reached for the baby bottle of honey water and dribbled some into the side of her mouth. She drank and swallowed with effort. She was coming to. I wanted to yell and awaken the whole house, but I thought it would frighten the poor thing. I would wait a bit longer to see if she moved anything on her own.

Gently, I scooped her up and put her head on my chest. I had heard somewhere that a wounded animal would heal faster simply by feeling the regular breathing and heartbeat of its mother or another animal. She could use my rhythm now . . . she already had my heart.

It was early in the morning, and the sun was just rising over the driveway and spilling into the bedroom through the opened drapes. I lay on my side and watched her face. She licked her mouth and her lips, as I gave her more honey water. Her eyes were glazed and only partially opened, but I thought she was trying to see me. Then she would close her eyes and start to sing again. I would stroke her and keep a gentle hand touching her. Within the next hour or so, I felt her legs twitch and her neck stretch a bit. It was a good morning.

Today, months later, I sit at my desk writing of my heart-wrenching experience with a drowned animal and all the people who became involved in the attempt to save her. But as I type, I'm reminded of the present world by the pawing at my elbow. I turn and look into those beautiful brown eyes searching my soul with such love and devotion, and at the same time wanting just a bit more of my attention . . . just a bit more . . . maybe a lifetime. This perfectly healthy animal, a survivor from the sea, is now the mistress of the manor.

"Hi, Missy."

This old scavenger surely found a precious treasure on the beach that day, a gift offered up by his lifelong love, the ocean.

The Gift of Trust

By Jon Wong

When I first met "the girls," they weren't happy dogs. My girlfriend, Jan, had inherited the two middle-aged miniature schnauzer sisters, Daisy and Franny, when her dad, and then her mom, had died a few years earlier. Since her parents' deaths, Jan had struggled to find the time to give her new dogs the attention they craved while trying to handle estate issues, a new dental practice, and her grief. But despite her best efforts, the two sisters, lacking interaction with other people and dogs, soon became standoffish.

I'd been finishing my periodontal residency in a neighboring state when I met Jan at a conference. As our relationship deepened, I heard all about the dogs, but when I first flew down for a long weekend to visit, I wasn't too excited about meeting them. I liked *big* dogs, dogs you could thump on the side and wrestle with, dogs like the German shepherd and Akita I'd grown up with.

Initially, Franny and Daisy did nothing to change my opinion about small dogs. Franny seemed interested in nothing but her next meal and lounging in her bed. Daisy was positively antisocial, growling and giving me the evil eye if I walked within two feet of her. They mostly ignored me—until lunchtime rolled around. When Franny smelled my roast beef sandwich, I suddenly had a new best friend. Determined not to miss a single luscious morsel, she began appearing whenever I ate. I was amazed at her bionic hearing. If the fridge opened, she would materialize, circling me like a tiny, gray shark. As the weekend passed, I found myself warming to little Franny, despite her size. I enjoyed scratching her stiff, upright ears and petting her seal-smooth gray back and soft pink belly. It was a different dog experience, but it was growing on me.

Over the next six months, I visited Jan often. Each time I showed up, the dogs seemed happier to see me. I knew I'd finally been accepted the day I drove up and was greeted with the "family bark"—a high-pitched, excited screaming known to schnauzer lovers everywhere—rather than the "stranger bark," a ferocious yapping in a lower register. The acceptance was definitely mutual.

Though Franny and Daisy were small, they had huge personalities. I got a kick out of the sisters' expressive ears, eyebrows, and tails. Sometimes they wagged those stubby appendages so hard they couldn't walk! After I finished my residency, I moved in with Jan, and I continued to work with the girls, eventually teaching them to walk on a leash, ride in the car, and come—though not reliably—when called. Daisy would fetch a ball for as long as I was willing to throw it. Franny loved to catch the treats I tossed her and would sometimes stand up on her hind legs and twirl around, trying to nuzzle the biscuit out of my hand before I threw it. They learned to enjoy our companionship. When Jan and I watched TV, Daisy would walk over to Jan for a scratch.

Franny, on the other hand, would wait until I stretched out on the couch, leap up, and settle onto my chest, sighing contentedly.

Things had settled into a comfortable routine when we began to notice that Franny wasn't always catching the treats—sometimes she lunged in the completely wrong direction. Within a week, we saw that she was bumping into things. She seemed more subdued, too, not her usual lively self. The local veterinarian, unable to find anything wrong, referred us to a veterinary ophthalmologist three and a half hours north of us. After talking it over with Jan, I made an appointment, canceled my patients, and loaded Franny in the car for a special road trip. Franny was in seventh heaven; she curled up in the heated passenger seat, got her own queen-size bed in the hotel room that night, and generally loved having "Daddy" all to herself.

In the morning, Franny took a turn for the worse; she couldn't even see me wave my hand in front of her face. Confused, she sat still, whimpering quietly until I touched her. At the vet's, she pressed against me through the whole exam. Whenever she heard my voice, she would reach her nose up to try "bonking" me on the nose—one of the tricks I'd taught her. Her anxiety only increased when she missed her unseen target. As we were waiting for the test results, she began to shiver and whine. The news was as bad as it was final: Franny was completely blind, the victim of SARD, an incurable, irreversible genetic disease that completely destroys the retina in a short period of time. The silver lining was that she was in otherwise great health.

Shaken, I left the office holding Franny in my arms, the doctor's last words echoing in my head: "Some dogs can't psychologically adapt to this change and have to be put down." On the long drive home, I became determined to help her as best as I could.

Over the next few weeks, Franny displayed all the symptoms of full-blown depression. And Daisy, instead of becoming the loyal guide dog as I'd hoped, made things worse. When poor blind Franny got in her way or mistakenly ate Daisy's treat, Daisy turned on her, snapping and growling. Soon, Franny spent most of the day in bed, preferring to sleep rather than leave the safety of her bed. She was giving up.

Jan and I searched for information about helping dogs cope with sudden blindness. We thought that if we could build Franny's confidence back up, she'd be willing to try to navigate this strange new world. We read about a woman who wore a bell to make it easier for her dog to find her. I tried it, despite feeling ridiculous, but Franny didn't make the connection. Then Jan remembered that Franny had always listened for my footsteps around the house. I started wearing flip-flops everywhere I went. Sure enough, Franny immediately began tracking the slap, slap, slap of my feet, following me around the house. What amazed me was how precisely she tracked the sound: if I walked five steps straight ahead and then turned and walked three steps to the right, she didn't just come toward my final position; she walked five steps straight and three steps to the right, too. I taught her the words, "careful," "step up," and "step down," to help her navigate steps, curbs, and uneven surfaces.

Within a week, I could tell that Franny was feeling more comfortable getting around the house. She had stopped bumping into walls and, most impressively, could circumnavigate the kitchen island at high velocity when the refrigerator door opened. I even got her to jump onto the couch again if I patted the cushion to help her aim herself toward the right spot. The day she stood up on her hind legs and twirled excitedly for her treat, Jan and I knew our Franny was back and that she would be all right. Today most people who meet her can't even tell that she's blind.

I didn't realize quite how much Franny meant to me until recently, during a conversation with a new business associate. This man and I didn't have much in common and had already exhausted most small-talk topics—the weather, his kids, and so on. I was telling him about Franny going blind and all that Jan and I were doing to work through it with her when he shook his head sadly and said, "Sometimes we just don't know when to put our animals to sleep."

I felt a surge of white-hot anger, but I refrained from knocking his block off. I told him that people had it all wrong when it came to special-needs dogs. "Franny isn't a burden or a drain," I said. "Far from it. What she gives me is more than equal to what I give her!"

I thought of Franny walking beside me on her leash, following me around the house, and lying warm and relaxed on my chest—everything right in her world. How could I explain what it felt like to be the recipient of her devotion?

In truth, Franny is more loving than most dogs. She knows that I've been there for her during the worst time in her life and that I'll always take care of her. That deep connection goes both ways. When we go on a hike, I can't just think about where I'm walking, I have to pay attention to where Franny's going: Is she going to run into a rock? Is she going to hurt her paw? Is she going to trip in a hole?

It took a little blind schnauzer to help me see beyond myself and into the heart of things—and to understand that an incredible amount of love and trust can come in a miniature package.

Heart of a Champ

By Michael Martin as told to Mikkel Becker

Alone and terrified, the tiny puppy dodged traffic in a busy city intersection in Paterson, New Jersey. Only when you got close could you see that it was a beagle, the distinctive black, brown, and white markings were mostly obliterated by severe burns that covered the top of his head and back and much of his chest and legs. A chemical had washed across his body, leaving him with exposed raw flesh and dangling shreds of skin and fur.

The pup cowered in fear as John, the local animal control officer, squatted in front of him. When John lifted him carefully in his hands, the little dog howled in pain, his deep brown eyes gazing up at John, pleading for help. There was no way of knowing if it had been an accident or if someone had intentionally inflicted such cruel and senseless injuries on this hapless pup, but it was clear that he needed immediate medical attention.

Rushed to a local veterinarian, the puppy was found to have injuries so severe that, even with the most aggressive treatment, the vet could only promise a fifty-fifty chance of survival. The suffering dog's fate ultimately rested in John's hands. Should he spend a large part of his limited budget and give the pup a chance, or would it be better to end his pain?

"Start treatment," he told the vet, still unsure what to do. "I'll come back in the morning with my final decision." Over the course of a troubled night, John decided that if the pup managed to make it through till morning, he should be given the opportunity to recover.

The next morning, John sighed with relief when he was greeted at the vet's door by Marge, the director of Save the Animals Rescue Team II (START II), a local animal adoption agency, whom he'd alerted about the puppy's situation. She was smiling from ear to ear. "He's doing better and is even eating a little," she said. "This one's a fighter, a tough little guy, a champ!" Champ. The name stuck. The puppy had been given a second chance at life, and a name to help him fight for it.

But a difficult battle lay ahead. Even if Champ made it past the critical-care period, John knew he'd need long-term rehabilitation. Though START II was already raising funds to help cover the cost of Champ's veterinary care, John asked Marge if she knew someone who would take the little dog in, treat his wounds, give him antibiotics, and love him back to health. Marge immediately recommended a local foster home: mine! My wife, Janice, and I have taken in special-needs animals for over fourteen years. We agreed to give Champ a place to stay and the care he needed.

Even with all of her fostering experience, when Janice went to the vet's office to pick up Champ, she was unprepared for what she saw. She couldn't help but gasp in horror at the red, raw flesh that covered the puppy's body in place of fur. Yet, instead of backing away, my sweet wife's tender, motherly instinct took over.

Without hesitating, she reached down and, carefully avoiding his burns, cradled Champ against her chest, with tears in her eyes. The puppy still resting in her arms, Janice was sent home with hugs of encouragement from the vet staff, doses of antibiotics and pain medicine, and ointment for Champ's burns.

I was waiting anxiously at the front door when Janice carried Champ into the house. I'd prepared a cozy bed for the dog, a large crate lined with blankets in the living room. Janice carefully set the pup down in front of the crate, and Champ scurried inside and cowered in the corner, as if afraid of what might happen to him at the hands of a human.

Sitting cross-legged in front of the open crate door, I tried to soothe the frightened puppy with gentle reassurances. "We're going to help you get better, Champ. We promise we'll never hurt you," I said as I stroked an unburned patch of hair under the dog's chin. Champ seemed to understand and eased himself into a curled ball in the corner of the crate, where he lay watching me intently.

At the time, I was walking the long, hard road of recovery myself. I had only recently overcome kidney cancer when I was struck suddenly with a massive heart attack. Once I was back on my feet, I returned to my construction job, but due to heart complications the doctor ordered me to stop working. I had to go on disability, which, for me, was like serving a prison sentence. Time once spent actively engaged at work that I enjoyed now passed slowly, and I became depressed. It had only been a month, but my days were so empty that it felt as though my time on earth had become meaningless.

Now, with Janice at work, I was in charge of Champ's recovery. I dedicated myself to his care, spending my days comforting Champ and tending to his wounds. The poor little guy was still just hanging on to life by his tiny paws, and even though he was on medication, the agony caused by his injuries could only be eased so much. He cried often, yelping in pain when Janice or I gently applied cream to his burns, and even whimpering in his sleep.

It was clear from the start that Champ was wounded not only physically but emotionally as well. The vet told us that there were scars on the top of his head that had been there before the burns, indicating that he had suffered prior physical abuse. He was afraid of most people. Each time a hand was extended to pet him, Champ would shrink back in fear. Our attempts to coax him out of his crate with toys and treats had no effect; he would lie in the back corner of the large plastic enclosure, the only safe place he knew.

But Janice and I never let Champ's reluctance and fear affect the loving attention we gave him. I hand-fed him kibble and other treats and sat by his crate for hours. Some nights I even curled up with a blanket and pillow to sleep next to his bed. Every day we carefully pulled Champ from his pen to cuddle him, whispering soothing words. Yet, even though Champ seemed to trust us more each day, he would still scamper back to the safety of his crate each time we were finished holding him.

As time passed and Champ's burns continued to heal, he began to gain strength and move around more easily. He ate kibble more freely from my hands and put some weight on his once skeletal frame.

Then, one day, about ten weeks after Champ had come to stay with us, Janice and I were sitting on the living room floor a few feet from Champ's bed, visiting with a friend.

"Look, look!" gasped our friend, pointing.

We looked over to see Champ's face peering out from the crate, his eyes darting back and forth across the living room, as if trying to decide whether or not he should venture out.

"Come, Champ!" I said excitedly.

Champ took his first voluntary step out of the crate, his white paw tentatively touching the carpet. Tears welling in our eyes, we eagerly encouraged Champ to keep going. The next paw emerged, then came his still-healing body, then his back paws and tail. He did it! Champ timidly approached me, his tail ticking back and forth, as if to propel him across the floor.

"Come here, boy," I whispered, gently patting my lap. Champ paused directly in front of me and looked up into my eyes, as if weighing whether or not he could really trust someone; then, tail still wagging, he pulled himself up into my lap, tucked himself into a small ball, and closed his eyes in contentment.

That was the beginning of Champ's new life. He left his crate behind, preferring the living room couch where he loved to curl up on my lap. He seemed to feel safe and happy at last. With the passing weeks, he started to do more and more of the things dogs do: chomping on chew toys, chasing his tail, racing around the house, and begging for treats and belly rubs.

Though caring for Champ had given me a lift, I still felt lost without my job, and sometimes I had bouts of overwhelming sadness during the day. Now Champ became the healer. If he was on my lap when my spirits began to sink, he would stand up on his hind legs, rest his front paws on my shoulders, and cover my cheeks with doggy kisses. Champ's loving companionship proved to be a powerful medicine for me. The combination of his affection and his continued recovery gave me the boost I needed to realize that my life did indeed have worth and purpose.

When Marge at START II called to discuss finding a permanent family to adopt Champ, we told her that Champ had already found a home—with us.

If you run into me on the street today, it's guaranteed that Champ will be by my side. Although I'm still on disability, and Champ will always have more scars than fur, we refuse to let anything keep us from experiencing a full life together. These days, Champ and I devote our time to increasing awareness of animal abuse. We visit local schools and businesses where I tell our story to crowds of people. I want to show everyone that second chances are possible, and that the power of friendship and love is unlimited. Champ, once so timid, now stands eagerly beside me, staring out at the audience, tail whirling with excitement, and tongue ready to lick anyone who approaches.

Not long ago, I took Champ to a local pet shop to let people meet him. A twelve-year-old boy and his father stepped up and asked to have their picture taken with the hometown canine hero. Wrapping his arms gently around Champ, the boy told me that when he was six years old, the tops of his feet had been badly burned. He'd been hospitalized for ten days and still remembered the tremendous pain.

"I wanted to come see Champ because he knew what that felt like," the boy said.

Champ sat with the boy, lapping his face as though it were a dripping ice cream cone. When the flash went off, the shutter caught an emerging smile and stopped a tail in wild side-to-side motion.

Jazz Takes
a Victory Lap

By Teresa Rodney

Normally, knowing that a dog of mine was eligible for the American Kennel Club's national agility invitational would be reason to celebrate. I had no doubt that Jazz, my flat-coated retriever, would qualify, since the top five dogs from every breed are eligible. Jazz is among the top agility dogs of *any* breed—one of the fastest in the sport.

But when I heard that the invitations had gone out, I started checking my mailbox with dread. The competition was still months away, and by even the most optimistic of predictions, Jazz would be dead by then. All the veterinarians I'd consulted told me the same thing—cancer would soon claim her.

She didn't look sick; I wouldn't have known she had cancer if she hadn't fallen off an obstacle in competition and knocked the wind out of herself. Worried that she'd broken something in the fall, I'd taken her to a veterinarian to be checked out. Nothing was broken, but a tiny shadow on her x-ray revealed something much more serious.

I took Jazz from our home in Southern California to Arizona, where one of my best friends, who is a veterinary surgical specialist, removed part of Jazzie's lung. Back at home, Jazz recovered slowly but surely and held her own on chemotherapy.

By the time the envelope arrived, she was back in competition, a willing teammate always ready to run and never giving anything less than her best.

Still I had to wonder: should I enter her? The location was favorable. With the competition being held in Long Beach, less than an hour from our home, we wouldn't have to drive for days to get there or fly with her in an airplane's cargo hold. She could sleep in her own bed over the two-day competition, and if the stress got to her, we could withdraw and go home.

There were so many unknowns, including the one I didn't want to face: would she be alive in December? None of our veterinarians thought it likely. But Jazz wasn't even supposed to be alive now, so how could I count her out? Sitting at my kitchen table with the invitation in front of me, I realized that if I didn't accept, I would be giving up on Jazz. I had no choice.

I mailed in the forms and tried not to think about it as the months went by. Jazz was still doing her best, wanting to run as much as ever at every trial we entered. We didn't practice, and we didn't train. We just ran the courses for the joy of being together for as long as it could last.

Nothing lasts forever, of course, and strangely enough, it was this lesson—that someone you love may be gone before you know it—that had first brought me to the sport of agility.

I was here because of my dad. We'd always had dogs, but Dad took up agility when it was new, and he and his dog were both good at it, naturals at navigating the obstacle courses as a team.

I was happy to see him so involved, so happy.

I guess it's some consolation that he died doing what he loved, but I wasn't much consoled when I got the phone call—heart attack, at an agility class. One of those things, we're so sorry . . . and my dad was gone.

Just like that.

In my grief I made a promise to him that I would take his dog, Devon, and finish the agility title they'd been working toward. It was something I wanted to do, *had* to do, and in the doing of it I discovered that, like my dad, I was good at the sport, too.

I've been running agility ever since, first with Devon, and after he passed on, with my own dogs. But with Jazz I went to a new level. We ran the courses not as a person and a dog, but as one living being, moving together. A change in my body language—a drop of the shoulder, a flick of the wrist—and Jazz would fly over one set of jumps or drive through a tunnel. A shift in my body weight and she'd head in a different direction, over the A-frame or flying through the weave poles.

Now, as the date of competition approached, her strength and her speed were coming back. She sometimes seemed tired, but mostly she seemed like her old self. None of my friends said anything about the upcoming competition, and my husband and I never discussed it. No one wanted to ask, and I didn't want to say, but we were all wondering: How was Jazz doing? Would she make it?

With a couple of weeks to go, I started to believe that she really would. A friend called, wanting to fly down for support, and I hesitated. Can you make the ticket refundable? We laughed, but we only let ourselves engage in the black humor because one thing was now clear: Jazz and I were going to run at the national invitational, cancer be damned.

The entrants set up in the convention center the day before the competition. I chose a quiet corner to place a crate for Jazz to rest in. Then I walked around, enjoying the buzz of activity.

The rings were being set up, with bright AKC banners unfurled from the ceiling and blue carpet rolled out for the show dog rings. In our agility rings, black rubber mats would go down on the concrete for better, safer footing. Crews from Animal Planet were hanging lights, while other network staffers with clipboards and walkie-talkies were figuring out where the cameras and other broadcast equipment should go.

I wasn't worried about the cameras—we'd run at televised competitions before—but I didn't like the footing. Mats or no, concrete is a hard surface to run and maneuver on as quickly as top agility competitors do—especially for an older dog with half a lung missing and cancer still lurking in her system.

In the morning I would let Jazz decide if she wanted to run, and I'd abide by her decision.

We arrived at the convention center before dawn. I settled Jazz into her crate, had a friend pin our number to the back of my T-shirt, and walked the course with the rest of the competitors. We never know what the course will look like until the morning of the competition, and we walk it without our dogs to figure out where we will put our own bodies to help our dogs through the course more quickly.

At this level, a dog's too-wide turn to a jump could mean

precious fractions of a second lost, earning a qualifying score—
a clean run—but probably losing the chance for a spot among
the top teams. A handler's dropped shoulder in the wrong place
might send a dog to the wrong obstacle at breakneck speed, and
a dog like Jazz would be over that wrong jump before I could call
her back. Do that, and we'd be DQ'd—disqualified—no matter
how fast we were.

I like to win—who doesn't? But I knew we'd already won just
by being here. Not just because we'd earned our spot, but because
Jazz was now two months past any best-case prognosis.

I walked back and looked at Jazz, resting on the cushion in
her crate.

"Jazzie? Wanna run?"

She did. I slipped the lead over her eager head, and we set out
for the ring together.

"Run clean, run fast," we wish each other in agility, the sport's
equivalent of "break a leg" or "good luck." Jazz sat at the starting
line, a coil of energy waiting to explode, as I walked out in front
of her to get the lead I'd need to keep up with her.

And then we were off.

She flew over the jumps, cut the corners, pushed through the
tunnel, and left the weave poles trembling in her wake. I knew
my friends were watching, cheering, crying, and the announcer
was telling all who didn't know that Jazz was a cancer survivor.
I was aware of it all, but all I felt was Jazz.

I was her, and she was me, a single being for 20 seconds . . .
23, 25, 27:36 seconds. We had done it, clean and fast. A couple
of teams were faster that day, but we didn't care. Whatever

challenges lay ahead, we'd done this, together, and that was triumph enough.

EDITORS' NOTE: *As this book went to press, six months after competing at the AKC Invitational, Jazz celebrated her one-year anniversary of being diagnosed by taking a trip to the beach. Though she was only given six to eight months to live, she and Teresa are still running clean and fast.*

Jazz, a flat-coated retriever, is a world-class agility competitor who has outlived and outrun a grim prognosis of cancer.

The border collie is recognized as the Einstein of the canine world.

There's never a wrong time
for a game of fetch.

This whiskery dog proves
good things come in
small packages.

Adopt
Me

Many a lifelong friend has
been found in a shelter.

If there's one lesson we can learn from dogs, it's this: Enjoy the moment.

Labrador retrievers make great companions and working dogs.

A Mixed Marriage

By Liisa Kyle

Whereas I am a "dog person," my husband is a "cat whisperer." As such, our marriage has been pet-free for twelve years.

Imagine my surprise when Jean-Guy gave me a holiday coupon for a puppy! Before my tears had dried, I knew exactly what I wanted, and I promptly volunteered to raise a puppy for Guide Dogs for the Blind.

It might be easier to adopt a child: To be accepted as a raiser, one must run a gauntlet of meetings, evaluations, and interviews. One's dog handling skills are assessed, and one's home is inspected. There's the official bestowing of the *Guide Dog Puppy Raising Manual*—issued with the implicit instruction to bone up.

Six months later, when I finally received the call that the "puppy truck" was bringing me a yellow Lab named Mario, I danced around the house.

When Mario arrived, I cradled him, stroked his jumbo-size, mink-soft ears, and squealed with delight. I couldn't wait until Jean-Guy came home from work to meet our furry toddler.

What I'd forgotten was that in the insular world of my cautious spouse, anything new was to be handled skeptically. I saw the wariness in his eyes the moment he walked in and sized up the stranger in his domain.

Uh oh, I thought. I'd expected that Mario would be my sole responsibility . . . but it didn't occur to me that his presence might end my marriage.

From his lopsided pose on the floor, Mario looked up at Jean-Guy. The pup's kohl-rimmed eyes sparkled. His tiny eyebrows arched up, attentively. The tip of his tail began to tap, tap, tap the carpet in a tentative greeting.

"What a handsome hound," remarked Jean-Guy, completely disarmed. He scooped up Mario and ushered him past my astonished mien to give him a house tour.

"This is the den," he explained aloud. "The bathroom floor is nice and cool if you get too hot." Mario seemed to hang on his every word. His tiny tongue lapped at my husband's chin. The furrows of Jean-Guy's brow melted away. He was smitten, besotted, head over heels in L-O-V-E.

From that moment, Jean-Guy was a doting co-parent, sharing responsibility for Mario's training, care, and feeding. He attended every Guide Dog Puppy Raiser Club meeting. He phoned home during his workday to see how "our boy" was doing. Each week, Jean-Guy clipped Mario's nails, cleaned his ears, and brushed his teeth (with poultry-flavored toothpaste). He became addicted to *The Dog Whisperer* on TV.

Mario entertained us daily. He'd contort himself into yoga positions in countless stretches. Wanting to participate in every moment of our lives—be it drying our hair, scrubbing the floor, or playing Parcheesi—his little face poked into the thick of things. We couldn't step out of the shower without finding Mario sitting there, an attentive audience. He'd get tangled up in our pants as we donned them.

As the love and laughter swelled in our household, Jean-Guy ceased working late, preferring to spend time with the newfound "family vibe" of our happier home. Mario single-handedly cured Jean-Guy's workaholism.

Mario inspired Jean-Guy to approach life differently. An off-the-scale introvert, my husband is quite guarded with others. Social events render him paralyzed. But inherent in training a Guide Dog puppy are the frequent interactions with curious strangers. To my astonishment, Jean-Guy bantered easily with passersby, patiently explaining the training process. Proud of Mario and armed with countless charming vignettes of his exploits, Jean-Guy loosened up considerably in social situations.

A devout homebody, Jean-Guy had always avoided outings. Suddenly, he started scrutinizing the local papers for events that would be "good socialization experiences" for Mario.

"Look here. A classic car show! A hockey game! A reggae concert!" Thanks to Mario, Jean-Guy and I had the vibrant social life for which I'd always yearned.

And while it used to be like pulling teeth to get Jean-Guy to go on holiday, he welcomed vacations with our pup.

"Let's drive up the coast," he'd gush. "Mario will love the Redwoods!"

Whereas none of the twenty tactics I'd tried over the past twelve years had compelled my couch potato husband to join me for neighborhood strolls, he was keen to take Mario on walks, several times a day. Jean-Guy began swimming with our bowser daily. As the bonds between man and pooch grew, Jean-Guy's love handles shrank.

When Mario needed to visit another raiser for a few days, our house felt like a mausoleum.

"How did we ever live without a dog?" wailed Jean-Guy. Before I could respond, he'd marched to the video store to rent *Lassie* to tide him over during Mario's absence.

Soon thereafter, Jean-Guy came home wearing a new T-shirt. It read, "My Lab is smarter than your honor student."

"It's official," I pronounced. "You're a 'dog person.'"

When he was old enough, Mario went to work with Jean-Guy three days a week. I couldn't help but notice that Jean-Guy's job satisfaction improved substantially, once Mario was installed in his cubicle. Even his commute seemed easier, with his furry buddy riding shotgun.

Mario soon established himself as the work team's favorite member. Oh sure, he didn't do much. During meetings, he mostly slept at Jean-Guy's feet. But Mario made a point of offering a groan or a snore or a fart at strategic times—just enough to keep his colleagues amused. Further, Mario's presence served to soothe many tense coworkers when they most needed it.

"I know we're not supposed to touch Mario," moaned one frazzled woman. "But I really need a hug today. May I?"

"How could I refuse?" said Jean-Guy, recounting the image of his colleague sobbing softly into Mario's shoulder.

When we received the official letter recalling Mario for his final training, it hit us hard.

The farewell began at Jean-Guy's workplace. Jean-Guy's boss insisted on throwing a farewell fete for our pooch. At the appointed hour, dozens of coworkers pressed into the main conference room. Projected on the screen at the front was a continuous slide show of the guest of honor. Besides the hordes present in the room, people phoned in to attend the party virtually—calling in from across the country.

"Be a good boy," they crooned across the airwaves. "We'll miss you."

As a treat, Mario was given the opportunity—for the first and only time—to romp off-leash among everyone. His coworkers had never before seen the playful, social side of Mario. To them, he had always been that quiet, perfectly behaved pup at Jean-Guy's side, the cute Lab they weren't allowed to touch. Many got misty-eyed watching Mario dash around the boardroom, happily accepting hugs, pets, and scratches from everyone present.

Clearly one thing we didn't need to teach our boy was how to work a room.

All too soon, it was time for our final trip together, driving seven sweltering hours to the Guide Dog Training Center. We cried buckets.

On campus, the balloon-festooned sign welcoming us contrasted starkly with our tsunami of tears. Mario did his best to cheer us up, but he was baffled as to why we were upset. For him, it was like going to camp: So many dogs to play with! Each day packed full of games and activities and school!

We savored our final snuggles with our canine child. The tears, hugs, and kisses flowed unabated. It was a *long*, silent journey home.

Back at our tomblike house, I found Mario's puppy ID tag. I started to add it to his scrapbook but was inspired, instead, to slip it on Jean-Guy's key chain. The tears in his eyes brimmed over.

"Thank you," he whispered, fingering the tag gently.

The following months brought us little information, simply a weekly notification as to which of the ten training phases Mario had completed. Each successful milestone was bittersweet: we were proud of our boy's swift progress and increasingly aware that it was unlikely he'd be returning to us.

Eventually, we got "the word" that cemented our separate fates: Mario had been paired with a person and would be graduating a few weeks hence. He was going to be one of the only 40 percent of puppies in the program who become working Guide Dogs.

Guide Dog graduation is a huge deal, with oodles of people, cameras, speeches, tears, laughter, and excitement. It's kind of like a wedding, a bar mitzvah, and a convocation all rolled together. The heart of the ceremony is the ritual in which the raisers pass their pups' leashes on to their visually impaired recipients. An emotional event, the organizers are quick to point out the tissue boxes scattered around the venue.

While many raisers never hear a peep about their pups after graduation, Mario's recipient immediately issued us an open invitation to visit them in Washington State. Kevin is a public speaker and consultant who travels the country educating people about disability awareness. Photogenic, social Mario will therefore have a perfect job as an ambassador of access.

All this good news served to dilute what would otherwise have been a very painful weekend. Of course, we wept when we were reunited with our Mario—especially that first moment he saw us and smothered us with frantic, wet Lab kisses. We were shocked to behold the buff, brawny physique he'd developed in the five months he'd been in training. And we did feel a pang to see him already bonded and continually "checking in" with Kevin.

But this was alleviated by the pleasure of developing a friendship with Kevin, the pride of watching Kevin and Mario working as a team, the joy of having so many trainers pop by to bid farewell to the "top dog" in the class, and the sheer silliness of seeing Kevin and Mario posing in matching graduation leis.

When we bade Mario farewell, any sadness at separation was tempered by the knowledge that he would have a more purposeful life with Kevin than he ever would with us.

Given the emotional toll of my spouse's first-ever dog experience, I resigned myself to resuming life in a pet-free home.

Imagine my surprise then, when Jean-Guy asked if we could raise another Guide Dog!

"Of course we can," I stammered. "But are you sure you want to put yourself through that again?"

"Oh, I don't know. Don't you think we got more out of the experience than we put in?"

I smiled, thinking of the joy, health, and love that Mario had injected into our lives.

"One thing, though," warned Jean-Guy. "I'd like to raise another male yellow Lab."

That's how Elijah came into our lives. A brawnier, snugglier version of Mario, our new Guide Dog pup has an underbite causing him to resemble Marlon Brando in *The Godfather*. It's a quirky, constant smile that mimics our own these days.

Ours is a mixed marriage—a dog person and a converted cat whisperer—who are committed to raising Guide Dog pups for many years to come.

Unconditional Love

Love Lessons

By Traci R. Smith

Spooky Louise was a pound puppy, and to this day I am still unsure if I picked her or if she picked me. I was thirteen years old, and though we'd had other dogs in our family while I was growing up, this was the first dog I set out to choose as "mine." I had loved and enjoyed all our canine companions, but nothing compared to the excitement of setting out to bring home my very own puppy.

When we arrived at the shelter and were escorted into the kennel area, the first dog I saw was a shiny little terrier, as black as coal, miniaturized even further by the enormous pen she was in. She was bouncing up and down and hollering with all her might, and I fell instantly in love with her. My mom encouraged me to take a look at the other dogs and not to choose the first one I saw. Reluctantly, I walked around, my heart being tugged here and there, but I couldn't escape the feeling of connection to the boisterous jet-black pup that quite obviously didn't intend to take no for an answer. After the paperwork was completed, we were soon traveling home, a pile of licks and giggles in the backseat. I felt like I was on top of the world, and I think it's safe to say Spooky Louise felt the same.

She was a bright spot in my turbulent teenage life. My parents had a rocky relationship at best, and my dad and I were mixing about as well as oil and water. When I was younger, he and I were close and shared many loving moments. But over the years, alcohol had become more and more a part of his life, replacing the daddy I had known with one I didn't recognize. I became resentful and hardened toward him. By the time Spooky Louise came into our lives, our relationship had deteriorated to the point that we avoided being in the same room together.

Deep down, I think we both wanted to find a path to reconciliation, but that path was littered with hurts and blocked by resentments that seemed insurmountable. Pride had built a wall that neither of us was willing to tear down. We had lost all common ground, aside from one thing—we both were head over heels for Spooky Louise.

My dad and I couldn't help but share our delight at the antics of this little dog. When she got the rips and went tearing down the hall and around the dining room table and back again, there was no way we could keep from enjoying a good belly laugh together. When she trotted around in a perfect circle in an attempt to win a treat, we were on the same team, cheering her with a chorus of "good girl!" and pats on her head.

Though our relationship as father and daughter was almost nonexistent, this little canine kept us connected through the bond we shared with her. She doled out love in large doses to both of our hurting hearts, and in spite of the fact that my father and I seemed to be on opposing sides, she gave us both an equal portion of undying loyalty.

I couldn't have asked for a better friend than Spooky. She was always there at my side to help mend a broken heart. Her chocolate eyes were filled with understanding when it seemed as though the world was against me, and she was a warm presence when I felt alone.

Just as Spooky soothed my weary heart, I would often find her doing the same for my dad. Many times I'd find her lying at his feet getting a belly rub or sitting quietly next to him. Though my dad seemed hard on the outside, Spooky brought out his tenderness. I often heard him talking gently and softly to her, saying things that were just between the two of them. Her heart was filled with secrets uttered from both of our wounded souls.

As the years passed, my father's alcohol and tobacco abuse took their toll on his health. Eventually cancer caught hold of him with a grip that would not let go. Though I was grown and had left home, I returned to spend his last weeks by his side at the hospital. During those days, our resentments finally melted, and the wall between us came crashing down. None of it mattered anymore. The bittersweetness of finding our way to reconciliation with so little time left was almost unbearable. But I wouldn't trade those final days with my father for anything in the world.

All along, little Spooky had known what love was—simple, uncomplicated, free from selfishness and self-righteousness—and she'd tried to teach us. I'm so grateful that, in the end, we finally did figure it out.

Get the Paper, Lil

By Jacqueline Michels

For the record, I am not a morning person. If I have my way, I do not like to string together more than six consecutive syllables before noon, and, frankly, supercheerful, zippity-do-da morning people make me nervous. Truth be told, in doggy years I am almost 280, so give me a break.

All I want is the morning paper, a cup of joe, and a little peace and quiet before I join the proverbial rat race, making my mad dash into life, liberty, and the pursuit of happiness (generally) and financial gain (specifically).

These days, I am simply trying to be jolly for Lilly's sake. She's a chocolate Lab pup who's a ball of fire, and I have to keep up. So I start the coffee.

There she is now, exuberant in her every waking moment, currently thrilled to be pacing the wood floor. On the other hand—or should I say, on the couch—is my purebred mutt, a true-blue affection hound. She's still snoozing. What a wise old dog.

"Wise dog, Terra," I whisper—like that would matter. My pal is very hard of hearing in her old age. An earthquake could let loose, and I doubt she'd even do that doggy-growling-in-her-sleep thing. "Good Terra."

Lilly responds to the doggy talk and . . .

"No jump, Lil! Yes, I love you, too. No, no kisses."

I push "start," and while I wait for a hot cup of morning atti-tude, I fling open the front door and command, "Get the paper, Lil!"

Lilly bounds off the front steps, tail doing an estimated 119 rpms as she hurls herself headlong off the step and heads straight down the drive.

"Good girl!"

Then she spies it—the little stuffed rabbit toy that was buried during last November's great snow. Up in the air goes the bunny, then back down to earth—or more accurately, into the muddy puddle that once was known as my front yard. That's it. Now roll with it. That's it. Chew on the remaining perky ear.

One, two, three laps around the front yard.

I take a deep breath and remember what the book said, "Be patient. No serious training for the first year." She is just a pup.

Oh, it smells so good out here. Why does morning air smell so sweet and thick? Not a cloud in the sky.

I receive one once white, now gray, soggy, slobbered bunny . . . minus an ear.

"Good girl!" Lil's tail wags even faster.

I giggle at the thought that if that tail wags any faster Lil will be airborne. Clear the launching pad for takeoff!

Oh, she wants pets—"Good girl, yes!" Her paws are stretched out in front of her, rump high in the air, waggling. *If only I had a camera.* Scratch the posterior. *Yup.* Oh, *life is good.* "Life is *so* good, huh, Lil?" *Okay, let's take it from the top.*

"Get the paper, Lil."

Oh, goodie, goodie, goodie! Four legs, two ears, and a tail cat-apult enthusiastically, free-falling off the steps. *Yes! She's got it! She's headed straight for the paper. Yes!*

Oh, oh.

Circle.

Circle.

"The paper, Lil. Get the paper."

Three turns. Squat.

Oh well, at least she's potty trained.

"Good girl. Get the paper, Lil."

This time I remember to follow through by stepping forward with my right foot and right arm (like the book says, my "gun arm").

"Good girl. Good Lilly! Yes! That's it! Now bring it here, Lil . . . Lilly? *Lilly!*"

Round and round the yard goes the brown pup; round and round goes the local, national, and world news, encased in blue plastic. Now it's airborne—wheeeee!

If tails are to dogs as words are to humans, the tail is scream-ing, "I'm so happy, I'm so happy, I can't *stand* it, I am *so* happy!"

What's that? Chirping . . . a squirrel!

She points! *Look at that tail! Nice and straight.* My eye follows the dog, who has dropped the paper to try to follow the squirrel . . . up, up, up . . . the tree.

I step off the porch to intervene and smile at the nice neighbor driving by. *Oh yes, so glad I wore the big, red plaid robe and rubber boots.*

Squish, squish, squish.

One more try. Then I'm getting the paper myself.

"Get the paper, Lil!"

By the book, now . . . nod, point, follow through.

Straight at the blue baguette—there she goes. Score! She's got it! Paper secure in jaws, she's coming back to me.

"Good girl, Lil."

"Bring the paper, Lil."

"Bring it here."

Folly, frisk, and rumpus. Up, up, up in the air so high, Lil tosses the paper. Then she gives me the I'll-give-it-to-you-if-you-chase-me-for-it look.

Six laps.

Wave at three smiling—no, holding-their-sides-while-they-drive-by-laughing—neighbors.

"Yeah, you have a good day, too!"

"Good girl, Lil."

Snatch the paper. Six more pets as Lil tries to grab the paper back.

"No," I say, but I fail to sound cranky. "I have it now, and I'm not giving it back."

"Yes, I love you, Lil . . ." Kisses . . . "Good girl, Lil!"

"Go get the bone." Lil fetches the bone without hesitation.

As I blow-dry the front page, I glance into the living room and see that Terra is still snoozing on the couch. A smile crosses my not-a-morning-person face. The coffee's hot . . . zippity-do-da!

Beethoven

By Carol Kline

My dog stands outside the door, barking to be let in—for the third time in as many hours.

"Beethoven," I yell, "you can get in! What do you need? An engraved invitation?"

It turns out he does.

Beethoven, a shih tzu mix I rescued almost twelve years ago, knows perfectly well how to use the dog door, but lately, he seems to have forgotten. He'll stand, ears up, expectant, barking short, preemptory barks—the dog equivalent of "Yo!"—alerting me in no uncertain terms that he is out and wants to be in.

I walk to the door, which is half glass, and look outside. All Beethoven has to do is push through the dog flap. But there he is, staring at the door, looking like a disgruntled restaurant patron waiting for his soup. *Waitress, what's the holdup here?*

Sensing my presence, he looks up. Our eyes meet.

"Come on, Beethoven. Come!" I say in that high, excited voice dog trainers tell you to use to encourage canine learning.

He looks at me, still expectant, but makes no move to enter.

I nudge the flap with my foot. "Come on in, Bay-bay! You can do it."

He looks at the flap and does a little shuffle, shifting quickly from paw to paw and back again. It's the same motion he makes when I lower his filled food dish to the floor or grab his leash from the shelf. *I'm ready*, he seems to say. *Bring it on!* But still he stays outside.

I nudge the flap open a little wider and call him. He looks fixedly at the flap for a few seconds, and then something must click inside his little dog brain, for he suddenly pushes through it. Just inside the door, he dances again, pleased with himself, then play-bows before making a beeline for the water bowl.

I sigh. We have entered the old-dog stage of life.

Beethoven has never been an easy dog. I took him home from the shelter where I volunteered because he had a behavior problem: whenever anyone reached down to pet him, he would snap. He never bit anyone, but it wasn't a habit that endeared him to potential adopters. I thought I could work with him and cure him of the unwanted behavior—and I did. With enough loving and petting, he stopped snapping at hands. But it became clear that he had other problems; he sometimes became aggressive if you tried to take his food or toys from him, so in the end, I decided that he'd be best off with me.

They'd named him Beethoven at the shelter because he looks like a miniature Saint Bernard—but one who'd been mixed with a Pekingese, judging from his underbite and bowed front legs. He had a tough-guy swagger and a tendency to dominate. I figured it was a cross-species form of small-man complex. Still, his spaniel-like brown eyes, expressive ears, and black mask were adorable. And he is the only dog I've ever had who actually hugs me. When I come home from a trip and kneel to pet him, he stands up on his hind legs, places a front paw on each side of my neck, and nestles his head against my throat, all the while emitting little moans of delight. It's the marshmallow side of our Danny DeVito dog.

Now, at fourteen going on fifteen, he is losing his doggy marbles. His black mask has turned to gray, and his eyes are cloudy in a certain light. He spends a lot of time snoring on his bed beside my desk.

Yesterday, I brought him home from the vet where he'd had an exam. We pulled up in front of the house, and when I opened the car door for him to get out, he hesitated, looking down, and then up at me. *Was the ground always that far away?* It was clear that he didn't feel comfortable with the jump. He kept staring at me, calmly waiting for me to solve his dilemma. So I picked him up, all twenty-eight fur-covered pounds. And instead of flailing and squirming as he usually did, he seemed as relaxed and comfortable in my arms as my stepdaughter had been as a toddler, riding easily and naturally on my hip.

Inside the house, his relief at being home was palpable. I sat down on the floor and stroked his soft brown ears, rubbing the places I know he likes. All evening, he followed me around. As I made the bed, he lay near my feet. I had to be careful to step over him as I moved around, tucking in sheets, spreading blankets, and placing pillows. He never moved or flinched as my feet went over him, back and forth numerous times. I marveled at the total trust he had that I wouldn't kick him or tread on him by mistake. For a few moments, he followed me with his eyes, and then he closed them. Sighing, he rested, content. He knew where I was and where he was. All was well.

What is there to do in the face of such devotion and dependence? Nothing and everything. I can only watch, his willing servant and his protector, as he makes his slow way down the path of old age.

And, of course, I can be there to remind him how to use the dog door.

For the Love of Leah

By Betty Sleep

I t's quiet as I sit working at the computer. No nails clicking on the floor, no rustle of paper being purloined from the recycling box, no cold nose under my armpit. I am lonely, despite the television in the background and the cats chasing each other over the furniture.

The hardest part of having pets is the fact that someday they leave you. When I retired from breeding golden retrievers, I was left with three dogs that grew old together and passed away one by one. Years ago I had decided that when they were all gone I would adopt a rescue dog, a throwaway nobody wanted. Now, lost without the companions that had kept me company through the writing of my first children's book and the breakup of my marriage, I decided I would look around. Just look.

To browse through the dozens of golden retriever rescue websites and Petfinder.com is to beg for heartache: abandoned dogs, amputees, blind dogs—beautiful, noble white faces without a home or anyone to care for them. It wouldn't hurt to ask. Maybe.

I was surprised by how keenly I felt the disappointment when I learned that in my region of New Brunswick, Canada, very few rescue dogs come into the hands of the local breed group. The next nearest groups or shelters were at least eight hundred miles away, and none of them would ship a dog. As I searched a wider geographic area, I discovered that, despite the many years I had spent breeding, showing, and training goldens, and the many glowing references I had, the response from these groups, when I got one, was "Sorry, you're too far away." After years of watching the proliferation of backyard breeders and providing input on cruelty laws, I understood that these rescue groups did have the best interests of the dogs at heart. But I was surprised that all of my work and dedication, both to my own dogs and to the ethics of dog breeding and ownership, weren't enough. I began to wonder if I would ever have a golden again. Briefly, I toyed with the idea of a puppy. But I had a feeling, perhaps a paw on the shoulder, that somewhere there was a dog that needed me as much as I needed him or her. All I had to do was find that special one.

In my web surfing, I came across a golden retriever message board with hundreds of members who were owners, breeders, or just people who loved the golden. I decided to post my story under the rescue section, asking if anyone knew of a group or shelter that would let me have a dog. Once more I offered my credentials and said that I would be willing to pay shipping and other expenses to save a dog. I found sympathetic ears, and at last, someone who would help.

"I don't know what I'm doing wrong," I told Jenna, a member from Florida who had placed several animals through private adoption.

"You aren't doing anything wrong," she said. "I will get you a dog. I don't know when, but I will find one."

The very next day, the dog found her. A neighbor called and

asked Jenna if she would take an eight-year-old golden retriever whose owner had died. The dog, named Leah, had been passed to a young relative, who had been trying to find her a home for a month and was about to dump her in a shelter. Older dogs surrendered by the owner are often the first to be euthanized. Jenna asked if I wanted her. I said, "Yes!"

In the next few days, the online world produced the web equivalent of the murmur you hear when news is passed through a crowd. A virtual whisper rippled around the board as Jenna and I posted back and forth about whether or not we could fly Leah to me. We decided not to since she would have to be crated for twelve hours for the trip.

The ripple swelled to a wave, and word came that members wanted to help get Leah up to me from Florida. The previous year a rescue golden had found its way to Washington State thanks to board members who organized a flight and contributed to its cost. This time, they wanted to do more. They were proposing a doggy train north, passing Leah from one member to another. But were there enough people to cover the nearly nineteen hundred miles?

The messages were flying. Who could meet where, and when? What day would we start? The stages of Leah's journey fell into place as if there were an unseen hand directing it all. Six days after taking her in, Jenna set off from Tampa, Florida, on the first leg of a journey that would take Leah through nine states and the hands of a dozen people, all the way up the coast to Calais, Maine, where I would pick her up. The dog nobody wanted became the dog everyone wanted to help.

I was a nervous parent. With nothing to do but wait for each connection to be made, I decided to create a website that would chronicle Leah's journey, both physical and spiritual, for it encompassed both of those things. Once unwanted, she was now on a trip that had become a priceless demonstration that love and compassion do exist and are extended sometimes simply for the joy of it, without expectation of anything in return. The website (www.fortheloveofleah.com) became her scrapbook. Each post, each photo, was an affirmation of love and caring, as can be seen in the smiles on both the humans and the dog.

On Monday, January 14, 2008, I picked her up in Maine, from Rob, the final angel in the train. It was a surreal moment, with Leah no doubt in shock from the change in weather, and me still barely believing the way everything had fallen into place.

Leah came with baggage, as so many rescue dogs do. Her lineage wasn't pure, which didn't matter as far as I was concerned. She had an ear infection and worms, and she had been on a poor diet and was overweight. While sweet and affectionate, she was also so sensitive that a raised voice would make her drop to the ground and grovel. Sometimes she would wake me with her nightmares—not the rabbit-chasing twitch of a happy dog, but a spasm of terror that would leave her shaking. With no idea of the cause, I could only offer comfort. She had no idea what a toy was for and appeared to have never seen a dog treat. It takes time to teach a dog to be a dog, let alone a friend and companion. I welcomed her into my world, and gradually she is letting me into hers. We are still feeling our way, reaching out to each other to make the final connection in the long road home for Leah.

Now, as I sit here at the computer working, there is a pile of old gold beside my chair. I swivel around, and she looks up. And what I see is the face of love.

Three Times Unlucky

By Rachael HaileSelasse

I t was mid-July, the height of the rainy season in Addis Ababa, the capital city of Ethiopia. Home to nearly seven million people, the city also harbors countless canines, eating, fighting, and breeding to maintain their place as wild urban animals in the metropolitan hierarchy.

Life for a dog in Ethiopia usually means being born onto the streets and beating the slim odds of survival in circumstances of hunger, disease, and predation. Wild hyenas haunt much of the city at night, and the dogs who manage to stay alive are vicious contenders and members of scavenging packs.

The rainy season arrives in Addis Ababa with daily torrents that have no equal, even in my famously soggy home state of Oregon. The rain washes the jumbled city of tin shacks and new high-rises to a slick, black shine and gives the surrounding hills and gum trees their electric-green radiance. Sewer canals and roadside paths merge into one toxic mixture of mud and garbage, and mother dogs can be seen toting their babies by mouth to higher ground, evidence of the flood's effect on their dens.

When I moved to Ethiopia to live with my husband, who

grew up there, I knew the culture would be different from the one I was used to, especially when it came to the treatment of animals. After years of working in shelters as an advocate for animals in the United States, I accepted that I would have to embrace a less active role. Observing the desperate lives of the dogs in the streets, I would tell myself, *This is just the way things are here.* I felt I had to understand my new home before I could attempt to act in it.

One evening, my husband and I were out on our nightly walk. The rain had ceased and the iridescence of the city in the evening was spectacular. We were taking our familiar neighborhood route, when I glanced toward the roadside and saw something flicker. There, next to the rivulet of storm water, was a slimy ball with piercing, black eyes. I stopped abruptly. "Is that a dog?" I gasped.

It was. The puppy, the size of a small woman's shoe, was hardly discernable, lying belly up. I couldn't walk away from those eyes, in what were clearly their last moments. We *had* to do something.

I could see the fleas crawling on her and smell the street stench, so I picked up a tattered plastic bag and then reached down to the puppy. She tried to squirm away, but her weak movements gained her only an inch. I scooped up her body, which weighed less than a pound, and swaddled it in the plastic.

Now what? My husband and I were beyond busy. We were only days away from our ceremonial wedding and were hosting five international guests who were in the country to attend. We were also preparing to move to another city in Ethiopia sometime in the next month. How could we factor in dog care?

We tried to give the puppy to a nearby shoe cobbler who was

working under a tarp-tent, but even with our offer of money, we couldn't entice him to provide the dog with shelter. "Someone threw her there in the last hour," he explained. "Besides, it is female and . . . black." Three strikes of misfortune had condemned this limp, soaking creature: being a dog, being female, and being black—the color of bad luck, signifying death, in Ethiopia.

We carried her back to our family's house, debating the whole time what to do with her. I brought the puppy into the bathroom as my Ethiopian in-laws stood staring in amazement and disgust. Only my husband's brother Tesfu came forward to help us, bringing a bucket of warm water and a small towel.

I scrubbed the puppy, who I judged to be about five weeks old, with soap and picked the insects off her, including the colonies between her nearly hairless toes. She was mostly black but each paw was white. The little dog's body was swollen from starvation, her ribs like thin fingers holding the last of her fragile life. Her fur was missing in patches and continued to fall out during her bath. Being bathed took all of her energy, and she slumped into a wearied sleep, still and no longer shivering. We dried her and wrapped her in the towel and then placed her in a cardboard box. "She might not live. She could be really sick," I said to my husband, "but we can just try this."

An hour later, I nudged the puppy to wake her. She raised her little eyelids as if they were heavy doors. I offered her a bottle cap of yogurt, but she didn't want it. Dipping my finger in it, I pushed the white paste gently into her mouth, onto her dry tongue. She swallowed. I did it again and again until the cap was empty. She fell back into slumber.

Every hour that evening I repeated the process, finger-feeding her droplets of yogurt and water. The next morning, she licked the bottle cap clean herself, and by lunchtime, she was eating small bites of mashed banana, only to drop her head back onto her towel, exhausted, and sleep again. After four days, she was licking her mixture of banana, yogurt, water, and breadcrumbs from a tea saucer. Every few hours we returned home to feed her and always found her huddled in the safety of her cardboard box. She was recovering—starvation, patchy fur, and all. Something in her eyes said: *I'm gonna make it, and you're gonna help me!*

Still uncertain of her fate and her place with us, I wasn't sure I wanted to give her a name and get attached, but a name came up spontaneously. As our Ethiopian family saw her improving, they often remarked in Amharic, "She is so *lucky!*" My husband and I agreed; in her last moments on the street, she had engaged me, a foreigner unfamiliar with the norms that doomed her. Without meaning to give her a name, we were already calling her Lucky.

We were almost packed up and ready to move when I suddenly came down with an infection and raging fever and had to have my appendix removed. When I returned home from the hospital, ten pounds lighter and very weak, Lucky had grown strong and was now capering around our guesthouse and chewing on squeak toys. With her fuzzy black-and-white coat and small, pointed snout, she appeared to have border collie in her ancestry. During my convalescence, our bond grew deeper. Now it was my turn to look at her and say, "I'm gonna make it, and *you're* gonna help me!" There was no question now of Lucky's leaving us; she was ours.

As soon as I was able, we began taking walks on the cobble-stone alleys outside the gates of our family's home—Lucky taking her first steps as part of the pack with my husband and me. All around us, the city was bustling with pedestrians walking to work, young women returning from the markets with baskets or sacks of fresh fruit, children kicking soccer balls, and elderly pilgrims on their daily route to church. Our trio always caused heads to turn our way, not just because I was a foreigner, but because little Lucky was a domestic dog walking submissively on a lead by our sides.

On those first brave walks, Lucky and I took it slowly, tackling first one alley's length, and then two, and then the neighborhood circle that amounted to the length of an American city block. I gradually recovered and gained strength, and she did, too. By this time, Lucky had grown from the timid, teacup-size lump we'd found at our feet to weigh almost three kilos (a little over six and a half pounds). One month later, we were able to move to Lalibela, a small town famous for its twelfth-century, stone-carved churches, about five hundred miles north of Addis Ababa. There, my husband and I would operate a tourist hotel.

In Lalibela, the three of us would walk down the road, an extraordinary sight in that rural part of the country. The little puppy lifted her coal-black head with pride, eyes shining, as her white paws flicked up and down like the hooves of a tiny, trotting horse. At first, the local children and their parents were afraid of our dog, palming stones as we approached or raising their walking sticks to strike her. However, the more daring boys and those consumed by curiosity began following our family pack. I was often asked if I'd brought Lucky from America because she looked so different from an Ethiopian dog: healthy, flealess, and full of joy.

The word spread, "Foreigner and famous dog, Lucky, walk daily!" and soon everyone knew her name. Before long, we had "regulars," children who joined us on our strolls and took turns holding Lucky's lead.

Lucky went everywhere with us, tromping across barley and flax fields, weaving through the town's neighborhoods of stone and mud homes, even climbing up narrow trails to reach plateau altitudes of over nine thousand feet. She greeted adoring tourist groups who cooed at her in Japanese, German, and Spanish. Sometimes, she took herself on walks. We lived in an apartment on the hotel grounds, and if we got distracted during a game of fetch out in the yard, she would take off on her own. Her pointed ears plastered back, Lucky would race down the hotel corridor and straight through the open doors of the restaurant. Customers would shriek or laugh as she ran from table to table meeting as many people as she could until I caught up with her. Scooping her into my arms, I'd hold her belly-up like a baby, laughing as she looked up at me with her flipping tail and sparkling eyes.

One evening my husband and I walked Lucky through a soccer field full of children playing in the setting sunlight. We decided to join the game and, tying Lucky to a nearby tree, we approached the group of children who were kicking a ball made of tightly wound fabric, remnants of old socks, and string.

We'd been playing for a little while when I noticed that Lucky had a special friend. A boy, perhaps ten years old, was sitting at the trunk of the tree with the half-grown puppy in his lap. She had turned her face up to him, and he was speaking softly to her and petting her. As I watched, more children began gathering around and reaching for her, until dozens of hands were stretching out to touch her. We discovered that the boy had told the other children that to touch Lucky was . . . good luck! Now everyone wanted to stroke that shining black fur.

After we were finished playing, we fetched our puppy from her place of honor and went walking back along the soccer field toward home. One of the children kicked the ragtag ball in our direction, and Lucky's lead slipped out of my hand as she dashed toward the ball and caught it in her mouth like a champion. Holding her head high, her white-tipped tail waving like a flag behind her, she pranced proudly across the soccer field. Everyone erupted in a chant for her: *Lucky! Lucky! Lucky!*

Though three strokes of misfortune had landed her on Addis Ababa's streets, our little dog had now become the mascot of luck and friendship in her new home of Lalibela.

A Shadow to Lean On

By Bill Mullis

It's dark in the long driveway, but the stars are brilliant. I stand beneath them, as I do every night, enjoying the quiet, settling my mind for sleep. Up the hill, among the bushes and young pines, in a place we still call the "puppy playground," a darker shadow rustles softly and glides down to me.

Bo is a black Labrador-Dalmatian mix, and I can tell where he is in the darkness because I've learned to look for the void where normal shadows should be. His coat, which glistens almost blue under the sun, reflects nothing at night; he is a black hole under the stars, a singularity from which moonlight doesn't escape.

He came to us by accident, rescued from a neighbor who didn't want him, who tied him out to an old bicycle using a length of cable for a chain and a plastic tie wrap for a collar. He was a five-month-old bag of doggy smiles with feet the size of horse hooves and the appetite of a young tyrannosaurus. I didn't much want another animal, but my wife, Amy, pointed out that the lanky, ebony puppy was already looking up to me as his "pack-Daddy" and reminded me about a dream I'd had weeks before, of a big black dog in the shadows beneath the old chinaberry tree, watching and waiting.

Even at six months, Bo was ridiculously strong. I was the only one in the house who could take him on walks, and he tried hard to pull me off my feet. Life was new and fresh, and there was so much to do and see. I tried to see it through his eyes, but I couldn't. All I could think about was how on earth we were going to manage such an unmanageable animal. We signed him up for the first available training classes at the local pet store and gritted our teeth. Secretly I fantasized about dumping him off on some unsuspecting soul. Every day it was some new disaster: Bo had knocked over the trash can; Bo had tripped somebody; Bo had jumped on the kids and scratched them.

A ray of light broke through our gloom even before classes started. It was on a drizzly, cold night after a series of rainy days. Much of the landscape had turned to that special kind of mud you get in the Southeast—when red clay gets saturated and turns into a cross between quicksand and wet concrete. Amy had gone up the road embankment to retrieve the cat, and on the way down she'd sunk into a mud pit up to her ankles. While she was trying to save her shoes, the mud oozed in and covered her feet. She tried to work her feet free and almost fell over. She could feel the strain on her ankles then, and with nothing to hold onto for balance, she was afraid she'd be stuck there till I came home, which might be hours. It was cold and dark, and she was scared.

Then Bo arrived on the scene. He was about fifty pounds then, half of which seemed to be in his paws. He looked his mom in the face, looked at her feet, then came around to her right side and planted those enormous paws where the ground was firmer, and waited.

Amy put her hand on his shoulders to steady herself, and after a few minutes of effort, she was able to free herself and her shoes from the muck. Bo walked her down the embankment, not leaving her side until they got back on firmer ground. After sniffing her to make sure she was all right, he went back up the hill to herd the cat to safety.

Amy was crying when she told me the story later that evening, and I looked at that gangly mutt more closely. *It's going to be all right*, I decided. There's a purpose here.

Puppy classes came and went, and Bo walked with me down the dog food aisle to get his diploma. We got him settled down, learned how to channel all that energy, taught him not to jump. He's still a puppy and will be for a long time to come—rambunctious, flighty, easily distracted. But he always knows when we need him, and he's always willing to take on that extra burden.

Now, a year later, the shadow looks up at me with glistening brown eyes, telling me it's time to go in. The January nights are cold, and he worries about my health. As we draw closer to the porch light the shadow takes form, and the face that looks back at me is smiling.

celebrating
the Bond

Riverwalking

By *Christine Albers*

T he Snake River, appropriately named, winds its way
through the countryside, meandering back and forth,
slithering east and then west, flickering and reflecting light
across the land. I amuse myself coming up with snaky terms as
Bud and I stroll along the riverside.

It's autumn. Summer lasted so long this year that fall took us
quite by surprise. Suddenly, cool, crisp air arrived, bringing crim-
son and golden leaves that slowly float down from the trees,
coating the river.

I'm like a little kid, skipping along, throwing rocks into the
water, totally bananas over Bud, my German shepherd pup, my
new best friend. I never had a dog before, so I follow him, content to let him tug and pull at me, sniffing his way along the
riverbank, jumping over rocks and driftwood, running through
piles of fallen leaves.

I pause. Bud pauses. Silence. The air is so cool, so fresh. We
sniff and drink it in. I look up from the view of Bud's tail curling
happily in front of me, and I'm awestruck by the tall evergreens
and the beautiful maples, oaks, and birches now turned orange,

lemon, saffron, and coral. My heart swells with joyfulness.

"I thank you God for this most amazing day," for this wonderful companion, who I rescued from a six-foot chain. This little doggy who ran away over and over again from his captive life in the neighbor's yard across the street, desperate for freedom, for companionship, for love, often dragging his chain and his stake behind him. A few weeks ago he planted himself on the front porch of my pink Victorian home and simply refused to leave. A brief neighborly negotiation, and that was that; now he's mine.

I love to see my Buddy boy happily running along the riverbank. Such a handsome dude, black and tan, with rusty, soulful eyes. He's all guy. And it occurs to me, I bet he's a fella who likes the water. I snap off the leash and we trek down a little closer to the water's edge. Though it looks cold, the sun is warm on my back. Bud pounces into the water with reckless abandon, jumping through the water and back up onto the sand, and then he plunges back into the river again. Do I imagine he is laughing? Such glee! I laugh right out loud every time he shoots into the water, so full of life.

The river flows endlessly, snaking in and out. The cool breeze touches my face. My dog, my happy pup, jumps in and out of the river. The mist gathers on the far riverbank and softens the bright fall colors. My favorite line from "Jabberwocky" wells up. "Oh frabjous day! Callooh! Callay!"

Surely, this is why God made rivers.

A Circle Unbroken

By *Linda Mehus-Barber*

As I gently drape a handful of soft dog fur on the boughs of our cedar hedge and drink in the perfume of springtime blossoms, my thoughts drift back to the beginning of this yearly ritual—to the year when I learned about the fragility of life and about hope eternal.

For fifteen years, my standard poodle, Toby, had been my constant companion. After my divorce, she had filled the emptiness left behind when dreams of love had evaporated like wisps of fog. During the day, she'd pranced along beside me with the high strut that comes with pride of pedigree, and at bedtime, she'd curled up beside me, keeping me warm during cold winter nights. Her presence brought joy and dulled the pain of those lonely days.

The winter of her life began slowly—a moment of forgetfulness, an accident on the carpet, an untouched bowl of food—but during the first warm days of June, Toby's winter descended with the full fury of a prairie blizzard. During those days, we were seldom far from each other, and on this particular day, she curled up in the shade of the apple tree, her soft brown eyes watching every move I made. I set down the bouquet of lilacs I had gathered and called her to me. She hobbled over and looked up with pleading eyes. Kneeling down, I rested my chin on her curly head.

Eight-week-old Wolfie, hardly bigger than a softball, tried desperately to get Toby to play, but today the old dog ignored the puppy's antics. Two weeks earlier, when I first brought Wolfie home, it had sparked something in Toby, and she sprang to life. She would wag her tail and grin as the little terripoo climbed over her. But now no amount of coaxing could get her to play. There was no denying that Toby's life was ebbing away. I wondered when the vet would call with results from the urine sample I had dropped off the day before.

Toby desperately needed a haircut but it was clear that she was in too much pain to go to the dog groomer. I began the arduous task of clipping her with scissors. There is a lot of fur on a standard poodle, and by the last click of the scissors, my backyard was white with clipped curls.

It was late afternoon when the call came. "Toby's results are in, and I am afraid it isn't good news." My heart sank as Dr. Bradshaw continued, "Her kidneys and other organs are shutting down."

We had discussed the options when I dropped the sample off. Now the vet's words echoed in my head . . . *nothing we can do . . . toxins in her body . . . poisoning her brain.* I knew it was time. Choking back tears, I loaded Toby into the backseat of my Subaru, then climbed in behind the wheel. Thoughts swirled in my head . . . *I can't let her suffer. . . . It's the right thing to do. . . . What if I'm wrong? . . . She is fifteen; that's ancient for a big dog.*

I pulled into the parking lot, then opened the door to help her out. Slowly, she limped along beside me, and for the first time ever, she did not struggle and pull away as we approached the front door of the animal hospital. Somehow she knew this visit was different. I glanced up at the receptionist, and she motioned me toward the waiting room. My heart grew heavier with each moment. The ticking of the clock echoed inside my head as the minutes dragged by.

Finally, Dr. Bradshaw came toward us, her face grave. "Are you ready?" she asked.

I nodded.

Toby and I followed her into the sterile room. I bent over and lifted my dog onto the cold, chrome table, surprised by how light she was. She lay down, her head resting on her forepaws, seemingly ready for what was to come.

Dr. Bradshaw looked at me. "You're staying?"

I nodded. I could not bear the thought of turning my back and walking away—I imagined her sad eyes following me, and her spirit crying out. *Where are you going? Don't leave me.* Instead, I wrapped my arms around her neck and buried my face in the downy softness of her fur. I could feel her heart beating, and it seemed in unison with my own. I did not watch the needle go in, but a moment later, I could no longer hear two hearts beating. Toby went limp, and I sensed the life leave her. My stoic facade crumbled, and salty tears soaked her fur. I kissed her and stroked her lifeless body. With one final embrace, I choked out my last good-bye.

The drive home seemed endless. Tears flowed in torrents, and the road disappeared in front of me. On autopilot, I somehow managed to navigate the route, until finally I pulled up to the curb in front of my house. It looked deserted, empty, lifeless. One step at a time I willed my legs to carry me into the house and out into the backyard. My new puppy needed me.

I opened the kennel and a chocolate-colored ball of fluff bounded out demanding my attention. As I played a little tug-on-the-sock with Wolfie, I happened to glance across the yard. I knelt in silent wonder as I saw three baby robins teeter precariously on the white picket fence. Mom and Pop eyed me suspiciously as they coaxed their babies to stretch their new wings again. I felt a shiver of excitement, knowing that I was likely watching one of their first flights out of the nest. As the spring breeze danced over me, I realized that new life surrounded me—the fledglings, apple blossoms, lilacs, unfurling leaves, and Wolfie. I closed my eyes and absorbed the glory of the moment.

Toby had passed on to another place, but enduring hope took my tears and sprinkled them on the garden of my soul. I saw Toby, a spring in her step, playing at the gates that I would someday pass through, too. Until the day when I would walk the same road, I knew the circle would not be broken, and that the new life around me would fill the emptiness.

Dusk fell and I scooped up little Wolfie and made my way inside. As I leaned against the kitchen counter cradling my puppy and looking out over my backyard, a wave of peace washed over me. I watched as several sparrows swooped down and gathered beakfuls of the fur I had left strewn around my yard. Soon others followed, and by late the next day, not a curl was left. All that spring, I would listen to the birds call, and I would smile as I thought of all the nests in the neighborhood that were cozier because they had a little piece of Toby woven into them.

Fourteen years have passed since the day I lost Toby, and now it is Wolfie who hobbles over to stretch out in the shade of the apple tree. As I drink in the perfume of springtime blossoms and spread Wolfie's clipped curls over the hedge, I know that it will not be long until I have to wrap my arms around her little body and say good-bye. I watch as the chickadees and finches swoop down to gather her downy fur, and I wonder how many of the neighborhood nests will be softer this year because they are lined with a little gift from Wolfie.

A Life Lived Fully

By Gina Spadafori

Heather trembled with anticipation the first time she saw the Ochlockonee Bay, her high-pitched whine vibrating in my ear as I drove. We'd driven four long days from California to arrive at a simple beach house I'd rented for six months, a bargain in the winter off-season of north Florida.

Heather is my little slip of a retriever, a dog who's happiest when wet. For the next six months she'd test the limits of her happiness, and I'd test the limits of my tolerance for the constant, briny smell of wet dog.

I pulled the road-grimed minivan in behind the stilt-mounted beach house and opened the back to unload. Heather jumped past me and hit the ground running, my well-trained girl suddenly deaf to my commands as she headed for the surf.

"Heather!" I yelled, surprised at her disobedience. "*Heather!*"

She turned and froze for a second, her ears up as she considered her options. Then she flew down the sand strip and dove into the water.

"HEATHER!" I yelled again. It didn't help.

"I hope you're going to get control of that dog," said a gravelly male voice behind me. "How long have you rented for? We *live* here, by the way."

I turned to find a couple in their seventies considering me gloomily from the shade under their own stilt-mounted home.

"Six months," I said, smiling apologetically and walking over to introduce myself. "She's not like this; really, she's not. We've been on the road." I motioned to the California plates on my van and yelled for my dog again.

The wife sighed; the husband shrugged. And just at that moment Heather came tearing back and shook the water in her thick coat all over the three of us.

"Sorry!" I said, grabbing Heather's collar. "It won't happen again."

"I hope not," said the wife, as I dragged my wet dog toward our new home.

In this part of Florida—a quiet, relaxed place more in tune with the culture of adjacent rural Georgia than with big-city Miami or suburban Orlando—dogs often ran free on the beach despite the leash law, a situation not all residents found appealing, my new neighbors included. The permanent beach dogs, Cowgirl, a Rhodesian ridgeback, and Honey, a yellow Labrador, walked around with the studied nonchalance of models on a runway. The dogs owned the beach, perhaps because on most winter days they were the only ones on it.

Heather wanted to join this free-roaming canine club, but that didn't fly with me. A city girl uncomfortable with rural Southern traditions, I refused to turn her out to run and swim as she wished.

She went out with me by day under what turned out to be good voice control once she got used to our new life. At night I let her out on a long line to relieve herself just before bedtime. I just couldn't bring myself to trust her so close to the surf, especially since I couldn't see her black coat in the dark.

But her dark coat wasn't the problem when she disappeared. The dolphins were.

A couple of days after we arrived, I realized that our walks along the empty beach attracted the attention of the local dolphins. I don't know if they were curious or just plain bored, but they'd swim along with us, just a few yards out, cresting now and then as if to get a better look.

The first time I saw their fins I thought they were sharks (guess I'd seen *Jaws* a few times too many) and yelled at Heather to get out of the water. It was too late, and I held my breath as they circled her. When their cresting backs revealed their identity, I sighed with relief. They swam closer, interested in checking her out.

Heather seemed just as interested in them. Once I relaxed enough to let her swim with them, she'd dip her head into the surf to get a better look. She'd also try to follow them when, after a few minutes of playful circling, they'd turn suddenly and shoot out to sea. She'd swim after them a little ways, then head back in toward the beach, get her legs under her, and turn to face the water. She always wanted to see where they went.

"They're gone, Heath," I'd tell her, and then we'd walk toward home.

I don't know what was different the day she disappeared. It could have been the weather, cold and wild with rain-heavy clouds and winds so strong the sand felt like needles against my face. Heather didn't care, and she pulled against the precautionary leash I'd put on her as we left the house. I hesitated, considering the wind-whipped surf. She whined, and I relented.

"Stay close," I told her as I snapped her free, and then I realized how ridiculous I sounded. Did I really expect her to understand the danger?

At first she seemed to, running along the beach and flirting with the high surf, looking back constantly to check in with me. Then she jumped in and started swimming, strong and fast. I saw the dolphins cresting, and though I worried at the size of the waves, I figured she'd tire and come back in when they left, as usual.

But this time she didn't. The dolphins turned and headed out, and Heather swam after them, farther and farther until all I could see was her black head bobbing in the gray waves. She'd never been out that far before, and I didn't know what to do. I couldn't swim after her. I didn't have a boat and wouldn't know what to do with one in such weather if I did. I yelled her name again and again, knowing she couldn't hear me over the din of the waves and sensing she wouldn't listen even if she could.

She was gone.

After a while, I realized there was nothing to do but go home and hope for the phone to ring after someone read the ID tag on her collar. I could only pray she'd be alive when that happened. As I headed back to the house, the clouds let loose a pounding, drenching torrent. I couldn't have cared less as the rain joined my tears.

The phone didn't ring—no surprise really, since no one in his right mind would be out on a day like this. I kept looking out the windows, hoping for a sign of her.

An hour passed. Suddenly I saw something black move, maybe a quarter-mile or more up the beach, a dot against the sand, quickly growing larger. Heather? Could she really be alive?

She could. She was running as fast as she could and straight for home. I dashed down the steps to meet her, crying as she circled me, both of us dancing at our reunion. Her face was the picture of canine joy, tongue lolling, and eyes dancing. *I'm back!* she seemed to be saying. *I'm back! I swam with the dolphins, and I'm back!*

"She's home!" cried the gravelly voice, the peevishness I'd known before replaced by grudging relief. "We thought she was drowned when we saw you walk back without her. You are so lucky, girl!"

My neighbors were once again standing under the deck of their home, and I could tell it wasn't rain on the wife's face—it was tears.

"I know," I said, still crying myself as I pulled Heather into my arms, not caring that she was soaked and salty.

The next morning found the clouds gone, the surf subdued, and no sign of the dolphins as we left the house. I was determined to keep her on leash for the rest of our time at the beach. She seemed to accept my decision and walked quietly beside me, not pulling or whining, head down and docile. Somehow, her behavior saddened me. As we walked back past the neighbors I could see them in the window, watching. What would they think if I let her go? If she swam out a second time and didn't make it back, wouldn't they think I'd killed my dog as surely as if I'd drowned her myself?

I paused, looking out into the bay and beyond to the Gulf where the last of the shrimping boats were heading in with their catch. And then, there they were, sleek gray backs and fins glinting in the sun, cresting as if they, too, were waiting for my decision.

Heather was looking at me, not the dolphins, questioning me. And I knew I could not force a dog happiest when wet to stay dry.

I closed my eyes and slid my hand down the leather leash until my fingers found the cool metal of the clasp. "Heather," I whispered as I let her go, a prayer for her safety. "Heather."

When I opened my eyes I saw the neighbors on their deck. I followed their gaze and saw Heather swimming out to sea. As we watched, she turned back far short of the dolphins and came paddling toward me, fast and strong while I waited on the beach anxious to hug my wet retriever.

Heather never followed the dolphins out again. She is an old dog now and most nights she moans in her sleep and moves her paws as if running—or perhaps swimming.

Since that morning when I made the hard choice to let her go, I have tried to live so that in my final days I, too, will have experiences worth dreaming about—like Heather's days of swimming, fast and strong, with her dolphins in the Ochlockonee Bay.

For many dogs,
life's a beach...
sometimes literally.

I think I hear the waves
calling me.

Always willing to
listen, some dogs
are "all ears."

This dog is very fashion forward—and a good sport.

Long legs come in handy when you're as curious as this Great Dane.

The Australian cattle dog—also known as the Queensland heeler—is bright, agile, and determined.

Internet dating,
canine style.

Two friends attempting a squeeze play.

Old Dog, New Tricks

By Mimi Greenwood Knight

Every picture I'd ever seen of my husband when he was a kid had a dog in it. I knew next to nothing about dogs myself, but I could tell they had been a wonderful part of his life. So, naturally, when we got married and moved to the country, I couldn't wait to surprise him with a puppy. I heard about a family who needed a home for their collie mix and snagged it for him.

Right off the bat, there were two problems with Blaze joining our household. One, he was the most hyperactive dog on the planet, and two, both David and I worked constantly, leaving Blaze home alone where he was forced to entertain himself by chewing on everything within a square mile and digging holes in the most inconvenient places. Each night when we returned home, he bowled us over like Dino greeting Fred Flintstone after work.

Then David left town for two weeks on business, and I knew I had to do something with our lonely, overly affectionate, ADHD dog. So I headed to the animal shelter, convinced that what our puppy needed to vent some of his energy was a buddy. I pulled into the parking lot, got out of my car, and met Biscuit. There he stood in his outdoor pen, a sturdy yellow Lab looking at me with eyes that said, *What took you so long?*

The woman inside asked if I'd chosen a pet I wanted to adopt. "No," I said, "but I think one just chose me."

When I told her which one it was, she made sure I knew that this was a ten-year-old dog. I thought, *That's good. We don't need another puppy.* With my lack of experience, I had no idea I was adopting a geriatric dog. As we filled out the paperwork, I noticed that a childhood neighbor of mine was listed as the previous owner. When I inquired about it, the shelter volunteer explained that this dog had belonged to my former neighbor's father. When he died, she couldn't keep the dog and was paying his board at the shelter in hopes that someone would come along and adopt him. Someone did.

When Biscuit and I arrived home, it took the two dogs all of five minutes to become best friends. I was worn out just watching them race around the yard together. I'd throw a stick into our pond, and the two would sail into the water and splash toward it, side by side. When they reached it, each would take an end in his mouth, and they'd swim, jaw to jaw, all the way back to shore, where they never tired of tugging it back and forth.

I couldn't wait for David to call that night, so I could tell him about Blaze's new buddy. When I did, there was silence on the other end of the line. But after I regaled him with tales of the two dogs' shenanigans, he warmed to the idea and looked forward to getting back to meet Biscuit.

During the next two weeks, I found myself trying to get home early from work, so I could enjoy watching the two dogs play.

Fetch in the pond remained their favorite game. Their swimming styles were a study in contrasts. Blaze churned up water for a foot on either side, working feverishly to keep himself afloat. Biscuit, being a Lab with webbed feet, glided across the water with barely a ripple, his legs moving indiscernibly under the water.

After a few days, I called my former neighbor to tell her I had her daddy's dog. She was thrilled and commended me for adopting such an old dog. Biscuit? Old? She talked about how she used to see him walking the neighborhood with her dad and laugh at how similar they were, doing the same "old-man shuffle." For a minute I thought we were talking about two different dogs, but as we talked, I realized that this was indeed the dog she'd left at the shelter.

Apparently, Biscuit had just needed the influence of a puppy to realize how much pup he still had inside. David and I worried that the newness might wear off and before long Biscuit would start shooing Blaze away, ready to settle back into his old-man lifestyle. No deal. He and Blaze were constant companions, wrestling partners, swimmers, and racers, and nine times out of ten, it was Biscuit who started the next tussling match.

I did notice some effects of his age though. The first few days I threw the stick in the pond, the dogs were equally frantic to swim out to it, so they could fight over it all the way back to shore. But after a while, Biscuit figured something out. If he stayed on land when I threw the stick in the water, he could let that young whippersnapper wear himself out doing all the work of hauling it in, where Biscuit was waiting to wrestle it away from him—the exuberance of youth versus the wisdom of age.

Biscuit lived for another six years—six healthy, happy, active years. Now Blaze is the old man of the family. His face is speckled with gray, and he naps more than he used to. When we go for a walk, rather than running up ahead and in and out of neighbors' yards for a sniff-fest, he's content to amble along beside me. I can't help but wonder what a puppy would do for him. Would it perk him up the way he had perked up old Biscuit? Would it add years to his life and life to whatever years he has left? I need to run some errands tomorrow, around the neighborhood where the shelter is located. I might just have to zip by there and see if anyone else is waiting to adopt me.

What's in a Name?

By Carol McAdoo Rehme

My "vintage people," I called them.

After six years of weekly sing-alongs, I knew and loved each frail resident at our local care facility. It was a place where old age was spelled L-O-S-S: loss of hearing, eyesight, and balance; loss of good health, manual dexterity, and physical ability; loss of mental acuteness, and—for most—loss of short- or long-term memory.

Yet none of that interfered with the joy we shared through music, laughter, and reminiscing.

At every session, I bounded in and greeted each person. "Hello. My name is Carol." I would always reintroduce myself, since names were especially burdensome for them to recall. Then I'd make a beeline for the grand piano that dominated a corner of the sunny lounge.

One spring Wednesday, I altered the routine.

"Look who I brought to meet you all." I held out a handful of ebony fluff. "Meet the newest member of my family. We call her Jazzy."

"Eh?"

I leaned closer to Wilbur's good ear, the one with the working
hearing aid. "This is Jazzy."

"Lassie?"

"*Jazz*-y," I enunciated.

"Sassy?"

"Jazzy," I repeated—louder. "She's a poodle."

"A puddle?"

"A *poo*-dle. A toy poodle." I grasped his withered hands, so he
could touch her silky head. Eight-week-old Jazzy stuck out a wet
tongue, lapped at Wilbur's bent thumb, and tucked her tiny head
beneath it.

"Ahh," Wilbur ducked his head and beamed. "I had me a dog
once. . . ."

And we were off on a tangent of remembrance. Everyone in
the room, it seemed, had a story to tell, a memory to share about
a dog that outsmarted and outshone any other.

So it was that Jazzy grew up under the loving ministrations of
the residents—and the new ones who replaced those whose
sojourn ended. They anticipated each visit, unhappy with me if—
heaven forbid—I had made an interfering appointment with the
groomer or the vet or had left Jazzy at home.

Like a favored grandchild, our little dog was praised, admired,
and doted on. She could do no wrong. Some of the residents
sneaked her treats—a piece of graham cracker or a crust of bread
hoarded from lunch. Others tempted her nearer with sweet words
and friendly pats. In time, Jazzy decided any empty lap was an
open invitation. Leaping from wheelchair to wheelchair, she took
full advantage of every opportunity to be fondled and stroked.

While we still sang and laughed and reminisced during the sessions, the focus and attraction of each sing-along had definitely shifted to this eight-pound lump of love. And it was never more obvious than one day when Jazzy eagerly raced ahead of me toward the lounge. With toenails clicking down the freshly scrubbed hallway, she skidded around a corner.

Lydia, a little wren of a woman, paused her walker to admire the streak of fur that whizzed by her. "Looks like Jazzy is here." She cocked her head in thought, "I wonder if she brought her friend."

"Carol," I offered a reminder as I followed Lydia into the room. "My name is Carol."

But Lydia wasn't listening. She was too busy digging in the pocket of her housecoat for a bit of cheese she'd thought to save from her lunch tray.

"Over here," she coaxed. "Over here, Jazzy."

Apparently, there are some names *everyone* remembers.

I Am *Not* Attached to This Dog!

By *Kimberly Ripley*

"Can we please get a puppy?"

I'd been asked this question many times by my three youngest children.

"No," I replied each time. "Daddy and I are allergic." It wasn't a lie. My husband and I are, in fact, mildly allergic to dogs. And cats. And horses. And dust.

"You're allergic to dust, and we still have dust," they would argue.

Ignoring this, I continued, "Dogs cost too much money. And they require lots and lots of time and energy—not to mention attention!"

"You pay attention to us—we require a lot of attention."

Yes, raising a large family did require lots of time and attention—and, of course, money, which was why a dog was simply out of the question.

But then twenty-year-old Scott, the eldest of our five children, moved back in with us after having lived 1,500 miles away for the previous sixteen months. Scott, who had never much heeded authority, had apparently grown tired of potential starvation, eviction, incarceration, and many other "tions." So he'd packed up his '94 Tacoma with all his worldly goods, including his D-O-G, and headed home.

They arrived at 1:00 AM on a Friday. I awoke to the sound of toenails on my kitchen floor. Certain that my husband had clipped his nails this fiscal quarter, I assumed the toenail noise signaled "the return." I greeted Scott with a fervor reserved for offspring and spouses following lengthy absences and gave the dog a friendly pat on the head.

And so we had a dog, a one-year-old, seventy-pound—and still growing—furry presence in our lives. Philly is part German shepherd, part Rottweiler, and a few unidentified parts as well. He immediately made himself right at home. Great with the kids, he never had a single accident on the floor, and he stayed out of the bedrooms and living room. Well, he did at first. Soon he began sleeping smack in the middle of my bed. Yes, to this day, I share a queen-size bed with a 250-pound husband and a sweet baby dog. (Did I just call him sweet?) Philly has developed an air of dignity as time has gone by. He won't ride in the backseat of the car, preferring the front, with the top down, thank you; he sits on the couch and expects a few bites at the table.

While some people might assume I've fallen for Philly, that's not the case. I've tolerated him because he's a guest in my house, and because my son's stay is only temporary. Besides, don't I have to at least be nice to him because he's sort of like a "grand-dog" or something? Scott and he will be looking for an apartment . . . soon.

Fast-forward a few months. Rents are awfully high in our area. And not too many places allow pets, which is why Scott finally took an apartment that didn't allow dogs. I guess that means Philly stays with us—just for a little while longer.

And that's okay. At least while he's here he'll enjoy the toys and the dog bed—and the dog run in the backyard. And he'll wear that adorable knit doggy coat when the weather gets a little cooler. Not that I care about his having nice stuff or anything. Those things were all on sale—except for his doghouse. That was almost $200. But I'd had a very lucrative week at work, so why not?

Last week was lucrative, too. So lucrative, in fact, that I booked all of Philly's aromatherapy baths for the coming year—complete with a plaid bow for his collar after his final brushing.

Hey, I know what you're thinking. And you're dead wrong.

I am *not* attached to this dog!

The Runt

By Marty Becker, D.V.M.

When the phone rang at 1:00 AM that summer night,
I knew it could mean only one thing: an animal
emergency.

Exhausted from several ten-hour days at my southern Idaho
veterinary hospital, I didn't even open my eyes as I pulled my
arm out from under our schnauzer, Bodè, and reached for the
phone. Keeping a commitment I'd made to myself upon my
recent veterinary school graduation—that I'd never make a person feel guilty for calling after-hours with a true emergency or
even a heartfelt concern—I engaged my upbeat daytime voice
and said hello.

On the other end of the phone was a young woman calling
from a pay phone, judging from the sound of cars speeding by.
(This was before the days of cell phones.) Breathlessly, the girl
explained that their Pekingese dog had been in labor for many
hours and was having trouble. The first pup's head was visible in
the birth canal but it wasn't moving with the contractions, and
momma dog was getting very tired.

"Would you please look at her?" implored the caller.

Honestly speaking, this is the kind of call that a veterinarian doesn't like getting at any time, let alone in the middle of the night. Not a regular client, calling from a pay phone —most likely too poor to have a phone in their home—about a very serious medical problem. But despite the potential problems of prognosis and payment, I agreed to meet them at the back door of my downtown hospital in fifteen minutes.

I had just opened the back door to the veterinary hospital when she arrived in a car that appeared to have been freshly plucked from blocks at a salvage yard. When she stopped the car and shut off the ignition, the car backfired loudly, scaring the daylights out of me. I was now fully awake, that's for sure!

The young lady I'll call Barb held a cardboard box that served as a pet carrier. Barb appeared to be about eighteen years old. With her thrift-store clothes and home-cut hair, she could have been a poster child for the trials of living in poverty.

I motioned for her to follow as I started turning on lights and putting on my smock. In the exam room, I looked into the cardboard box and saw a dog in serious trouble. Upon preliminary examination, the Pekingese, whose name was Peaches, had shallow respiration, gray gums, a fever, and a pendulous abdomen. I knew the huge pup lodged in the birth canal would be stillborn.

Lifting her out of the box and putting her on the exam table, I started Peaches on some warm fluids, which rehydrated her and helped her get over the shock. Then I set about facilitating the delivery of the dead pup. Barb kept caressing Peaches's honey-colored body and speaking lovingly in her ear. *No doubt,* I thought, *this young lady really loves her dog.*

Often, the first puppy in a litter is the biggest, and it's common for large-headed breeds like Pekes to have trouble delivering puppies. With some lubricant and repositioning I made a pull, and the pup literally popped out into my hands. Not only was the puppy dead, but the amniotic fluid that surrounded it was off-color with a bad odor. This didn't bode well for the mother's recovery.

Barb must have been watching my furrowed brow because she asked me if everything was going to be okay. I was honest with her, explaining that Peaches had blood poisoning and only a 50 percent chance of making it.

I carefully palpated the little dog's now much smaller abdomen. To my surprise, I felt two more pups still inside Mom, both the size of golf balls. Based on the condition of the first pup, I was sure they were also dead but didn't say anything to Barb.

I gave Peaches an injection, and minutes later she started having contractions. Without lifting her head off the table she expelled another stillborn pup, significantly smaller than the first one. After several anxious minutes, the last puppy was pushed out. Although fully formed, the puppy was Lilliputian, even by toy breed standards. I laid what would have been the runt of the litter on the side of the table and turned my full attention to Peaches's survival.

As I was tending to Peaches, I noticed a slight movement of the dead puppy's mouth. It was gasping for air! Alive! I immediately pulled the clingy matter from around its nose and throat. Hearing gurgling, which indicates fluid in the lungs, I began the standard lung-clearing procedure. Holding the pygmy puppy in my hands, I lifted it above my head and then swung it between my legs and back up again. I repeated the motion. On the third swing, the slippery puppy squirted out of my hands and slid across the exam room floor. Barb gasped.

Mortified, I picked up the tiny puppy and was relieved to find it was unharmed. But it still wasn't breathing properly. At that point, I literally breathed life into it with my mouth, as none of the oxygen masks I'd normally use were small enough.

Against all odds, both Peaches and Thumbelina, as Barb aptly named the pup, survived the night. Before dawn's light, Thumbelina was avidly sucking colostrum from Peaches's ample udder and Peaches was giving her the traditional motherly sponge bath with her tongue. Tears of happiness streamed down Barb's cheeks as she high-fived me for the apparent medical miracle that had been bestowed upon doggy mother and daughter. Both Barb and I had grins so wide, we could have eaten bananas sideways.

Before I even mentioned payment, Barb told me that she had no money to pay me but promised to find a way to take care of the bill—eventually. I'd heard that story before and never expected to see Barb or her money again. Like many veterinarians, I figured I'd done the work of a Good Samaritan, albeit one who still had student loans to pay off.

Imagine my surprise when, almost a year later to the day, in walked Barb with a perky Peaches, lil' Thumbelina, and a heaping plate of just-out-of-the-oven chocolate chip cookies. She handed me an envelope and asked me to open it. Inside was a card and a money order for the entire amount owed for that emergency call. Barb told me she had raised it by walking the sides of

country roads for months, collecting aluminum cans for the recycling fee. The inscription on the card read:

> Despite the fact I was a total stranger, you came to Peaches's
> aid in the middle of the night and saved her life. Not only that
> but, you brought Thumbelina, like Lazarus, back from the dead!
> ☺ You have my profound, eternal gratitude for what you did.
> We, in turn, have made a vow to harness this miracle and make
> a positive difference in the lives of others.
> Love,
> *Barb, Peaches, and Thumbelina*

Then Barb handed me a stack of photos from a local nursing
home where this interspecies trio was now doing weekly visita-
tions with seniors. In each of the pictures, I saw beaming faces
that, though aged, glowed with joy. Looking up, I smiled at Barb
and her two precious pets. Spreading love and happiness in this
way surely fulfilled the mission of harnessing the miracle of life.
They'd repaid their debt—and then some!

Love Everlasting

By *Marcia E. Brown*

"If Heaven is a place for love, who would bring more than pets that loved and were loved?" wrote my dad after he lost his cherished dachshund, Mamie. She had been his constant companion for eighteen years.

My mother also insisted that all her dogs and cats be part of any Heaven she was willing to enter.

I never knew if their concept of pets as part of the afterlife came early or late to them. It may have begun in a sweet experience we three shared after we lost the dog most finely attuned to our own psyches.

I named him Chandu. Half collie, half shepherd, he was my companion and best friend for the six years of his life, a mannerly dog of exceptional intelligence. Definitely a member of the family, he was seldom left at home when we all ventured out.

World War II was raging at the time. Housing was in short supply in our small Arkansas town, and we spent the war years in a small house at a busy intersection. Totally uninsulated, the house was a sweatbox in summer and so cold in winter that ice sometimes coated the windows on the inside. Over bare floors, my mother put down her handwoven rugs, with one especially for Chandu.

In summer, Chandu spent the long hot days in the cool crawl space beneath the house, often joined by his canine pals from around the neighborhood—in those days, most dogs ran loose. At night, all year long, Chandu slept under my bed.

We had no television, so reading was our main recreation. On Saturdays we stocked up on library books for the week. Officially, only guide dogs for the blind were allowed in the library, but Chandu's reputation for gentlemanly behavior won him special privileges, library visiting among them. Each week he walked with us up the long flight of stairs to the main floor of Carnegie Library to greet the librarians as old friends. Then he lay down just in front of their desk, facing the wide steps, and greeted all other visitors with a swish of his plumed tail. Clearly, he enjoyed a place of honor.

At home, most evenings Chandu reclined snoozing on the rug between my mother's chair and the couch where Dad did all his reading lying down. My small rocking chair was near Mama's lamp. Chandu often lay with his head resting on my feet.

Like most dogs, Chandu preferred routine and regular hours. He retired nightly at nine o'clock, my bedtime. It did not matter whether we were home or not: nine o'clock was bedtime for my shaggy pal.

Mama once wrote to a friend, "This bedtime routine embarrassed us when we had guests. To Chandu, Marcia's bedtime *was* bedtime, period. His withdrawal was so pointed that no guest could stay on and remain at ease. If we were visitors in another home, at nine o'clock Chandu arose from beside the feet of whichever family member he had chosen as companion while listening to the conversation and made the rounds of the room gazing meaningfully into each of his family's faces, his tail waving a 'Let's go!' Then he walked to the door, clearly ready to leave. This maneuver was repeated until it effectively dampened conversation, making our departure mandatory."

And then one day a speeding car abruptly ended Chandu's life on this Earth. We were all deeply saddened. A few days later, Mama looked up from her evening reading and said, "I heard Chandu walk through the house today."

Dad told me later, "I think your mother is imagining things because she misses having Chandu around all day when you're in school."

I nodded my head. I didn't know what to say.

One evening about a month later, when the room was still and we three were absorbed in our books, the clock chimed nine. We all looked up when we heard a familiar sound: a large dog's paws on the bare floor between the small rugs. The clicking of toenails was first heard near Dad's couch, then the sound moved across the room past my mother and me and stopped at my closed bedroom door. This was followed by a familiar scratching noise near the bottom of the door.

We looked at each other. Mama stood up and walked to the bedroom door. She opened it and stood aside. We heard the clicking across the bedroom floor followed by a scrambling sound of something moving under my bed. Then, there was silence.

Mama closed the door, returned to her chair, picked up her book, and smiled at Dad and me.

I cannot swear that I truly heard a ghost. But I do know with certainty what three people of independent minds heard that night. I might be willing to attribute that to shared grief except for another incident.

Our living room windows were low enough that Chandu had been able to stand on the front porch and look in at us. When he was outside and wanted in, invariably he first came to one of the windows, checked inside, and gave a little whine. Then he raced to the door to be ready when someone opened it for him.

The week after our mysterious experience, a friend of my mother's came for coffee. The two women were chatting but stopped talking when they heard the sounds of a large dog coming up the front porch steps. When a whine was heard, followed by the sound of paws hurrying toward the door, the noises were so clear and definite that Mama's friend got up and opened the door herself! The porch was empty.

That was the last time we heard such sounds. My parents and I listened. We wondered. Finally we told each other, parting at death is not really good-bye but *auf Wiedersehen*, "until we meet again," believing with all our hearts that love—human and animal—is everlasting.

Must-Know Info

Musf-Kñ♀w Iñf♀
Build a Better Bond with
Trick Training

Responsible dog owners take obedience training very seriously. A dog needs to learn not to jump on people because, besides being annoying, someone could get hurt. And dogs need to learn to come when called, so they don't dash out into a street and get hit by a car. Obedience training keeps dogs safe and ensures they are pleasant companions.

~⌒~   ~⌒~

But while obedience training is a serious responsibility, "trick training" is just plain fun. The owner can laugh, the dog can play, and there's no pressure. This fun carries through into any obedience training you and your dog do, with many benefits, including a better rapport with each other and clearer communication. In addition, having fun with your dog is great for your relationship. After all, all of us—people and canines—are more likely to repeat something that we enjoy doing. So if we have fun training, whether it's tricks or obedience, we're more apt to do it!

All dogs can learn tricks; which kind of tricks depends on the dog—his physical abilities and how quickly he thinks. Walter, a cockapoo owned by my friend Kate Abbott, is a whiz at action tricks. He spins, rolls over, shakes, waves, weaves through her legs, and does a hundred more tricks.

My Australian shepherd, Bashir, prefers tricks that make him think. He has learned the alphabet and will touch the right letter with his nose nineteen out of twenty times. Although tricks are fun, many of them can also have a useful purpose. Bashir will open the door for me when my hands are full—I know women who wish their husbands would be so helpful!—and he will go get the bucket and carry it for me to the goose pen when we're feeding. He seems especially pleased when there is a purpose for his tricks.

Some breeds have a physical advantage. Basset hounds will never be as agile as border collies, for example, but all dogs are capable of learning. Even old dogs can learn new tricks, despite the saying to the contrary. In fact, old dogs love new tricks, because they enjoy the attention and the fun of trick training.

"Shake" is probably the most popular trick people teach, followed by teaching a dog to balance a treat on its nose or to roll over and "play dead." Another fun trick that most dogs can learn quickly is to jump over an outstretched leg. Sit in a low chair and stretch one leg out in front of you. With a treat in one hand lead your dog by inviting her to follow the treat over the lowest point of your leg (your foot) as you tell her, "Lady, over!" When she steps over your leg, praise her, "Yeah! Good job!" and give her the treat. Do this two or three times, and then take a break. As she gains confidence over the next few days, move your hand so she's jumping over your leg instead of your foot. When she's jumping over your leg consistently and with enthusiasm, add some variety by asking her to jump over your arm instead. You can then curl both arms into a hoop and ask her to jump through your arms. It's all great fun! With this trick, and with all trick training, keep the training sessions fun. Use lots of rewards—verbal praise, petting, and treats, and don't be afraid to cheer for your dog's efforts. Keep training sessions short and sweet.

Don't work until your dog is bored, and always stop the training on a high note. Finish with something your dog can do well, so the training leaves you both feeling good about it.

Retrieving dropped items is a "trick" assistance dogs use frequently to help their physically challenged human partners. And many therapy dogs have learned "stop, drop, and roll" for demonstrating fire safety to kids at day care centers and schools. I've used Bashir's ABCs trick at day care centers, primary schools, and special education classrooms to motivate kids to read.

The most important thing to remember when teaching tricks is to have fun! There's no pressure with trick training: have fun, laugh with your dog, encourage her, and experiment with your training. The only technique to avoid is force, which takes the fun out of the training. Use treats and praise instead.

A group trick-training class is a great way to get started. The group assists and encourages each other under the trainer's direction, and you see what's working and what isn't. Most trick-training classes also finish with a little show, and that's always great entertainment.

The only limit on the number of tricks your dog can learn is the number of tricks you can teach. So get busy!

Liz Palika has been training dogs and their owners for more than twenty-five years in Southern California. She is a certified dog trainer, behavioral consultant, and an American Kennel Club Canine Good Citizen evaluator. Liz is also an award-winning author who has written more than fifty books on pets, including *The Complete Idiot's Guide to Dog Tricks* (2005). Her newest book is *The Howell Book of Dogs* (2007). For more information, visit www.lizpalika.com.

Musf-Kñọw lñfọ
Dog Driving You Nuts?
Help for Battling Bad Habits

Behavior problems can be life threatening, and in fact, more young dogs lose their lives to unruliness than to illness after their owners give up on them. Dog owners must recognize that prevention—in the form of consistent, positive training and socialization—is the key to having a well-mannered companion. The goal is to prevent problem behavior with early socialization and training, by rewarding the behaviors you do want, and by not making your dog fearful, anxious, phobic, or aggressive with punishment-based training.

～ ～

Training helps to give your dog a "human-preferred" outlet for his normal doggy behavior. When you provide predictable, immediate, and appropriate consequences, your dog can learn what you want from him, and choose those "good" behaviors over the "bad" ones.

Don't force your dog to live in fear of setting a paw wrong and being punished; instead, teach your dog what you want, and let him know when he gets it right. Always reward what you want instead of punishing what you don't want.

Now, on to some specific examples.

Begging: The easiest way to stop begging is to never let it begin. If you already have a beggar by your table, you've taught your dog (perhaps by accident) that begging gets her food and attention. Give your dog something else to do while you're eating—provide her with a food-puzzle toy or a chew toy stuffed with bits of treats or peanut butter. Never, ever reward begging. You should choose when your dog gets goodies, and those should usually be given in her bowl, in a crate, or as a reward in training.

Destructive chewing: Instead of just taking away what you don't want your dog to chew on, substitute something that's more attractive as a chewable object. Dogs play with toys that have the right texture, are new or different, or that have treats inside. Find toys that are tough but not hard—you don't want any broken teeth—and set them up so he is encouraged to work at chewing, such as by adding treats to toys or using food puzzles. Once you've offered your dog some attractive alternatives, prevent access to the items he was chewing on. Put shoes away, block off parts of the house that contain the forbidden objects, and use nasty-tasting spray deterrents, motion-detector sprays, or sound alarms to deter repeat chewing. But be fair—deterrents work best when you've provided alternatives. After all, chewing is a natural canine behavior.

Barking: Look for a situation where your dog's barking is low-key, when you can easily distract her, not when she's wound up and yapping away in a frenzy. As soon as she begins to bark, get her attention with food, say "quiet," and give her the treat for paying attention to you and interrupting the barking, however briefly. Eventually, she'll come to understand that you control her barking, and that a bark or two of alert is okay, but when you say "quiet," her job is done. When your dog is watching you, it's very hard for her to bark, especially if you have a favored treat or toy in your hand the first few times. For excessive barking, keep her on a leash and a head halter so that you can close her mouth on the word "quiet," and then release and reward for the calm behavior.

Jumping up: As with begging, you must reinforce what you want—and that certainly is not jumping up. Encourage and reward an incompatible behavior, such as "sit." Ignore the jumping up and focus on the behavior you want your dog to learn instead, such as "down," "sit," or "go to your mat." Turn your back on your jumping dog, ask for the behavior you want (such as "sit"), and then reward your dog when he sits. A leash and head halter can help to make your dog sit during practice sessions.

Come when called: "Come" is very hard to teach because each time the dog does not return it reinforces the idea that she doesn't have to. Typically the "come" command is taught with a dog on leash, and often with a treat. Ask your dog to "come" and encourage her in with praise and treats. Once she understands at a short distance, use longer lines, and practice with ever-more-difficult distractions. Three things that help in training a dog to come when called:

1. Never allow an untrained or partly trained dog off leash. It only takes one experience for a dog to realize that if she ignores you, you're not able to do much about it.

2. Make coming to you a good thing. Give your dog a favorite treat or toy when she comes so that she learns to covet the opportunity to get that reward.

3. Punishment is off-limits. Never punish a dog for coming to you, even if you've chased for a mile and cornered her, so she didn't have a choice but to step in your direction. If you punish a dog for coming to you, you'll be sure to put into her head the idea that the next time she's loose, it's best to keep on running.

Because teaching a dog to come when called can be so difficult, most pet owners would benefit from the help of a trainer or behaviorist, either in a private or group setting. A good trainer or behaviorist can set up a program that will help you to get through to your dog and encourage you to not allow your "kinda trained" dog off-leash—always a recipe for disaster.

Whenever you run into a problem with your dog's behavior, don't wait to tackle the issue, hoping it will get better or that your dog will outgrow it. Bad behaviors never improve on their own; in fact, they often get worse. Ask your veterinarian for a referral to a behaviorist or trainer who can show you how to turn your dog around—without harming the dog physically or mentally or turning your pet into an animal who may hurt you.

Gary Landsberg, D.V.M., is board-certified in veterinary behavior both in North America and in Europe. In addition to his general veterinary practice, Dr. Landsberg offers behavior consultation services at the North Toronto Animal Clinic. He is a frequent speaker on behavioral topics at veterinary conferences around the world and has coauthored a number of veterinary behavioral texts as well as a series of behavior brochures. Dr. Landsberg has also hosted his own TV and radio shows. He was awarded the American Animal Hospital Association award for his contributions to the field of companion animal behavior and is a past president of the American College of Veterinary Behaviorists. His website is www.northtorontovets.com.

Must-Know Info
Preventing and
Fighting Cancer

The best treatment for cancer is prevention. Cancer hits some breeds more than others—golden retrievers and Rottweilers, to name but two, and purebreds are considered more at risk than mixed breeds. Environmental factors such as exposure to pesticides may further influence the rate of cancer in dogs. When selecting a dog, consider adopting a mixed breed from a shelter, or work with a reputable breeder if you're choosing a purebred—one who is aware of the health problems of the breed and is working to reduce those problems.

Restrict your dog's daily intake of food to maintain a fit body weight throughout her life. Allow your dog to eat the required amounts recommended for her specific breed type and height, and adjust that amount according to how your dog's body responds. A fit and healthy dog will have a wasplike waist and a tucked abdomen. Feed a balanced, delicious, high-quality diet with limited amounts of carbohydrates (e.g., sugars), moderate amounts of good quality proteins, and higher levels of omega-3 fatty acids, such as docosahexaenoic acid (DHA). Cut down on extra calories by substituting vegetables such as baby carrots as treats or by adding volume to meals with green beans. If you prepare your dog's diet at home, work with your veterinarian to ensure it is balanced and nutritionally complete. Consider an omega-3 fatty acid supplement, which can be found in any health food store or even at most supermarkets and pet retailers these days, to enhance health and wellness and potentially reduce the risk of developing cancer. (Talk to your veterinarian for guidance on supplements.) Add regular exercise together, and both you and your dog will benefit with greater health and a closer, more vibrant relationship.

Spaying and neutering have been shown to be an effective method of preventing some cancers, especially those related to the reproductive system. Spaying has significant effects on preventing breast cancer if it is done before a dog goes into her first heat cycle.

Eliminate exposure to environmental carcinogens such as pesticides, coal or kerosene heaters, herbicides (such as 2,4-dichlorophenoxyacetic acid—read the label!), passive tobacco smoke, asbestos, radiation, and strong electromagnetic field exposure. Each one of these factors has been implicated in some studies to increase the risk of cancer in dogs (and in people, for that matter).

What if your dog is diagnosed with cancer? Most dogs who are treated for cancer, even those who cannot be cured, are still able to enjoy a high quality of life. Cure rates and quality of life are improving because pet owners are working with veterinarians to identify the disease early and employ new technologies that are highly effective in the initial stages of cancer care. In most situations, especially when the cancer is detected and treatment begins early, dogs undergoing cancer treatment experience limited or no decrease in the quality of life.

Almost all dogs with cancer can be helped. Here's what you need to know:

Get all the facts. You can defeat the darkness of cancer with knowledge. Work with your veterinary team to learn as much about the disease and its treatment as possible. Be proactive. Ask questions and obtain resources to eradicate the many misconceptions about cancer and cancer therapies. The Internet can be a powerful resource for seeking cancer information; yet be aware that there's a lot of misinformation out there. Work with your veterinarian to understand the validity of all information you obtain.

Pick a good team. You are in the best position to know and meet your dog's needs and desires. Your most important task is to find a veterinary team that is experienced in cancer care—ask your veterinarian for help—and committed to working with you as a member of that team. Once the right team is forged, everyone can provide true compassionate care. Compassionate care requires that your dog is as free as possible from the adverse effects associated with cancer and cancer care. This includes freedom from pain, nausea, and starvation. Ask what supportive care measures can be undertaken to enhance the quality of your dog's life.

Write things down. Record all discussions about your dog's disease or recommended treatments with the veterinary team. Repeat the information back to ensure you understand completely.

Seek support. Bring a friend or spouse with you when you talk to the veterinary team.

Include the whole family. All discussions should involve everyone who is intimately associated with your dog, including your children at their level of understanding (preschoolers, for example, can't comprehend death). Allow everyone to ask questions and voice opinions.

Understand there are no correct decisions, only decisions that are right for you. Do not worry what other people will think about your decisions. You know your dog better than anyone else in the world. Once you are empowered with the information you need, listen to your heart, and you will make the right decisions.

Gregory Ogilvie, D.V.M., is director of the Angel Care Cancer Center at California Veterinary Specialists and president of the Special Care Foundation for Companion Animals where he cares for patients and their families, teaches interns, residents, and veterinary students, and leads an active cancer research program. Prior to his move to Southern California, Dr. Ogilvie was a full tenured professor, internist, head of medical oncology, and director of the medical oncology research laboratory Animal Cancer Center at Colorado State University from 1987 until 2003. Dr. Ogilvie lectures to thousands of aspiring and graduate veterinarians and scientists each year and has been recognized as Veterinarian of the Year by both the American Veterinary Medical Association and the American Animal Hospital Association, among many other awards.

Must-Know Info
Shoot Your Dog—
With a Camera, of Course!

Digital photography has changed everything for the casual photographer. Instead of wasting roll after roll of film—or not bothering to take pictures at all because of the trouble and expense of getting them developed—it's now possible to take hundreds of pictures, happy in the knowledge that if there are just one or two good ones out of every few dozen taken, nothing has been wasted except possibly your time.

Even better, photo-editing software has made it possible to salvage a marginal image. With a few clicks of the mouse, the out-of-frame, out-of-focus, or just "not right" images are jettisoned forever. A few clicks more, and those images with potential are fixed up and made suitable for framing—a crop here, a reflecting eye changed to brown, the elimination of items cluttering up the background.

But the best pictures aren't made in a software program. They start with the knowledge of how to get great pictures at the first shutter click. Learn these basics and you'll end up with memories that will last forever:

Outside is best. Taking pictures outside gives your dog a more natural, healthy look. Dogs are bundles of energy. Learn to adjust your aperture and shutter speed to shoot objects in motion, or use the predefined program many cameras include, and you'll capture the best of your dog's athletic grace.

If your dog is a solid, dark color, use your flash to bring out the detail in her face. If you end up with "red eye" use photo-editing software (basic programs come free with many new cameras and computers) to fix the problem.

Get close. If you want a good picture, you need to go where your dog is. Shoot at eye level or just above eye level to get the best visual connection. Be careful not to get too low though. A dog's long snout, shot from too low an angle, can block the eyes, breaking the connection you're trying to get.

Watch your backgrounds. Think neutral—a plain wall, not a cluttered cabinet. Think contrast, but not too much—a lighter background for a dark dog, darker for a light dog. If your dog loves to curl up on his paisley dog bed, consider throwing down a solid-colored blanket before you shoot. You might be able to edit a distracting background later, but it's easier to avoid it in the first place.

Be patient. If your dog does something cute and you miss it, don't despair. Chances are, if you're patient and keep your camera ready, you'll catch the encore.

Get help. Children make the best photographer's assistants. Get a kid to help get a dog's attention with a toy or treat or by holding the dog for a picture. Nothing is more adorable than kids and dogs together.

Be creative. If you want to capture your dog kissing your child, do what the pros do: put a little butter on your child's cheek, and let the dog lick it off. Food is good for more than kissing—it's also great for getting your dog's attention for the shot. Squeaky toys and laser pointers work well, too. If your dog will stay for a few seconds, throw a toy (or even your car keys) in the direction you want her to look.

Have fun with software. The camera's just the first step to a great picture. Basic photo-editing software can do more than fix errors—it can turn your images into art! Play with colors, contrast, sharpness, and more, or use special effects such as "watercolorizing" to create something unique.

Keep taking pictures. Just as with children, people tend to take pictures of new puppies and then put the camera away. But your dog is always changing, and the images you one day love the most might be of your dog as a sweet senior.

So get out there with that new camera, whether it's a pint-size point-and-shoot or a sophisticated digital SLR. You'll never find a subject more enthusiastic than your dog, especially if treats are involved for good behavior.

Troy Snow is a professional freelance photographer whose work has been widely published and appreciated. Along with a team from Best Friends Animal Society, he went to the Gulf Coast in the aftermath of Hurricane Katrina to help animals and people. The stories from that rescue effort are told by his stunning photos in the book *Not Left Behind: Rescuing the Pets of New Orleans*. Many of Snow's photographs are on the Best Friends website (www.bestfriends.org), and you can see more of his work at www.troysnowphoto.com.

Must-Know Info
Get Going: Travel with Your Dog Has Never Been Easier— Or More Fun

So many dog-friendly places can be found these days that it might be easier to note what you can't do when traveling with a dog. With your dog at your side, you can explore beautiful parks and beaches, take spectacular hikes, stay at wonderful hotels or quaint inns, and enjoy tasty meals al fresco at myriad restaurants. You can also ride on ferries, gondolas, and trains, sip wine at vineyards, attend baseball games, cross-country ski, go to church, catch outdoor concerts, sniff out bookstores and art galleries, and go shopping at high-end stores.

One of the joys of traveling with a dog is that it's easier to meet people. Dogs open doors: most people are friendlier when they see you have a dog.

With all the dog-travel guides and dog-friendly businesses these days, it's easier than ever to plan a terrific road trip with your best friend. (Air travel, for all but the smallest dogs, means traveling in cargo, and that's really not a lot of fun. So this discussion will stick to road trips.)

Advance reservations aren't always essential, but they are

recommended. During busy times, there can be a dearth of hotel rooms for humans, and that's even truer for humans with dogs. But with a little planning, it's easy to find dog-friendly lodgings. Record numbers of hotels, motels, and inns in the United States are welcoming dogs. Many even provide doggy welcome baskets and other goodies that make you and your dog feel right at home. Books and websites provide a great way to find lodgings and other great dog-friendly spots, allowing you to research pet-friendly places to get a real feel for where you'll be staying.

The rules for traveling with your dog include:

Bring the right companion. Bring only a well-behaved, friendly, clean, flea-free, healthy, house-trained dog on your travels. Dogs who are dirty or ill-mannered can close doors for future canine travel companions.

Never leave your dog alone in your car. Even if it seems cool out, the sun's rays passing through your windows can heat up the car quickly, putting your pet's life at risk. The car can even get too hot for your furry friend when it's in motion, especially if your dog is in the rear of a hatchback or station wagon on a sunny, warm day. Plan to travel when it's not extremely warm.

Provide plenty of water. Make sure your dog always has access to cool water. Dogs on the road may drink even more than they do at home.

Take regular breaks. There's nothing more miserable than being stuck in a car when you can't find a rest stop and *really* need one. Imagine how a dog feels when the urge strikes and he can't tell you the problem. How frequently you stop depends on your dog's bladder and disposition, but you can figure that your dog needs a break about as often as you do.

Pack the essentials. The ultimate "doggy bag" includes your dog's food, bowls (including a nonspill bowl for car rides), bedding, a brush, leash, towels if you'll be in mud or water, a first-aid kit, poop bags, prescription drugs, proof of vaccinations, treats, toys, and your favorite dog-travel guide. (You can get water on the road, so bring a container to fill.) For a dog who sleeps on a bed with you, bring a sheet to protect the hotel bedding.

Play it safe. Make sure your dog is wearing a license, ID tag, and rabies tag. Having your dog microchipped before you hit the road is a good idea, too. Snap a disposable ID on your dog's collar, too, with a cell phone number and the number of the place you'll be staying locally; some people may not bother to make a long-distance call if they find your dog. (Paper key tags—available at any key shop or hardware store—are great for this purpose.)

Never leave your dog alone in your room. Leaving a dog alone in a strange place invites serious trouble. Scared, anxious dogs may tear apart drapes, carpeting, and furniture. They may even injure themselves. They might also bark nonstop or scare the daylights out of the housekeeper. Plan your travels well, and you won't be tempted to leave your dog in your room. If you just can't bring your dog along on an outing, many hotels offer pet sitting or can provide you with contact information for local sitters and kennels.

Follow proper "petiquette." This means:

- Don't let your dog bark when you're at a lodging or a restaurant.

- Always scoop the poop on your walks. Don't ignore it. You know it's there.

- Don't use the ice bucket as a food or water bowl. Gross!

- Yes, your dog needs to be clean. No, don't bathe him in your hotel's tub.

Plan ahead, stay safe, and be considerate, and you and your dog will always be welcome back.

Maria Goodavage is author of the popular thousand-page guidebook, *The Dog Lover's Companion to California*, and two other books in the Dog Lover's Companion series. Maria, a former *USA Today* reporter, is chauffeur to her research assistant, Jake, a yellow Labrador who has no driver's license—yet. They live near a dog-friendly beach in San Francisco with Maria's husband and daughter. Find out more about Maria and Jake's books at www.caldogtravel.com.

> # Must-Know Info
> ## Reduce Shedding and Keep Your Dog's Coat Huggable

A dog's coat is like a neon sign showcasing his good overall health or lack thereof. A great coat is shiny and parasite-free and has no excessive scaling or dander, no mats or abnormal hairless patches, no foul odors and is normal for the breed type. "Normal" varies from dog to dog, of course, because different coats are normal in different breeds, such as the cords of pulik and komondorok and the hairlessness of the Chinese crested.

The most common mistake dog lovers make regarding their pets' skin and coat is not grooming their dogs enough—of course, "enough" will vary by breed. And to a lesser extent, providing dogs with diets that are too low in essential fatty acids can also have an adverse effect on coats and skin. The proper grooming regime and a proper diet will go a long way to ensure your dog's coat remains beautiful. Proper grooming will also help alleviate what seems to be one of the biggest concerns of dog lovers: shedding!

To understand shedding, you have to understand the hair cycle. In dogs, hair falls out and is replaced by new hair in a constant cycle that is different from breed to breed, so the dog's coat always looks full. Even the "hairless" breeds grow hairs, but these are unhealthy and break off or are quickly shed.

In a normal dog, the hair is replaced as it is shed, so you never see a bald patch. What we call shedding is both hair falling out naturally and hair falling out before its time because of being disturbed, such as by the dog chewing, rubbing against things, or getting petted. Other causes of shedding include skin diseases and even chemotherapy. Hormonal diseases can cause hair to stop growing, and in some cases to not shed because of a lack of new hair to push the old hair out. In these cases the dog's coat appears thicker—at least temporarily. But as the hair stays on the dog too long, exposure to water, sun, and other elements cause the hair to become dry, discolored, and unhealthy.

While everyone wants a shed-free dog, there's really no such thing as a *non*shedding breed. Some dogs do shed less because they are genetically programmed to keep their coats longer before new hair pushes out the old. These include poodles, Afghan hounds, and many terrier breeds. In general, breeds that require clipping or have very long coats shed less. Short-haired dogs (like Labradors or Dalmatians) shed more because their old hair is replaced more frequently with new.

If you're looking specifically for a dog who won't shed much, get a small, long-haired dog and keep the coat trimmed short. Why? Because the hair of long-haired dogs falls out less frequently, and a smaller dog has less hair to shed than a large one. If you keep the hair clipped short, the hair that does fall out will be shorter and result in less volume to deal with. Most people, however, choose the dog they want and simply deal with the shedding that is normal for that breed.

Must-Know Info:

Products that promise to end shedding can't change the reality of normal growing and shedding of the coat. They don't decrease shedding; they just get you to groom your pet more frequently, which causes the hair to shed because of the friction. Petting, wiping down, and massaging are also grooming methods that create friction that causes hair to shed. The good thing about these methods is that the pet (and the owner) don't think of them as grooming!

Brush your dog's coat at least weekly with a tool recommended by your dog's breeder, a professional groomer, or your veterinarian. You can brush pets daily if you want to really take control of shedding; this removes the hairs that are ready to be shed and gets them on a brush or comb instead of your furniture.

While you are brushing, check for and break up mats by working in corn starch, cutting through the middle of the mat and away from the skin with sharp scissors, and then picking apart the mat gently with your fingers and a comb. Don't forget to check the fur between the toes of the paws!

Look for and remove plant material, such as burrs and awns, and if you see ticks, don't touch them with your fingers: use a tick-remover or tweezers or wear a rubber glove to remove them and dispose of down your sink. Having to remove a tick or two now and then is normal if you're out in the fields with your dog, but ask your veterinarian for prescription flea-tick preventive to help keep these pests under control.

As for the fur that "gets away," well, there's a reason those sticky rollers for clothes are a staple in every veterinary practice—

they work! Swiffers and other electrostatic products are great on wood, tile, and vinyl flooring. Try a lightly dampened sponge on furniture or car upholstery to pull the hair out.

What about bathing? Any dog who isn't bathed at least every month or so is going to develop its own unique body odor, which will vary greatly from one breed type to another. You'll want to bathe your pet as often as needed to offset the smell, using products designed for dogs, not human shampoo.

It's important to catch skin problems early. Too often, dog lovers don't notice a problem until hair loss, a rash, or sores are so bad they can't be missed. Watch for excessive skin flaking or a change in coat color and quality, and have any change in coat condition checked out by your veterinarian.

Taking good care of your dog's coat and skin will help keep your pet healthy and beautiful—and up that "huggability" factor.

Craig Griffin, D.V.M., is a diplomate of the American College of Veterinary Dermatology and the founder and co-owner of the Animal Dermatology Clinic. He is a frequent lecturer and clinical instructor of veterinary dermatology, and he has published many articles and books on small animal skin disease. Dr. Griffin has received the ACVD Award for Excellence for outstanding contributions in veterinary dermatology. The Animal Dermatology Clinic has four permanent locations: Tustin, San Diego, and Marina del Rey, California; and Marietta, Georgia. There are also eleven satellite clinics. The website for Animal Dermatology Clinic and Dr. Craig Griffin is www.animaldermatology.com.

Must-Know Info
The Dos and Don'ts
of Dog Parks

Dog parks or dog runs—fenced public areas set aside for off-lease play—are a great idea, but they're not ideal for all dogs. How do you know if your dog can benefit or should exercise elsewhere? Here's what you need to consider.

Your dog should be at least six months of age and must be fully vaccinated. That's because puppies don't have fully functioning immune systems, and dog parks are places visited by hundreds of dogs, some no doubt carrying a contagious disease. Dogs who are extremely old, chronically ill, or otherwise immune-compromised should also be left out of the dog-park experience. When in doubt, ask your veterinarian.

Not even a healthy dog can just be thrown into a dog park. Your dog needs to be socialized before setting paw in a dog park and should be friendly with other dogs and with people. (These recreation areas are not the best place to socialize your dog, since they can be overwhelming at first.) If your dog acts out in fear or aggression with other dogs, in new environments, with new people, or when in a confined area, then he is not ready for the dog park—and may never be.

Not all dogs can learn to play nice, and some perfectly good dogs just aren't well suited for the communal experience. Some dogs will unintentionally provoke fights or fearfulness from other dogs with overly aggressive or unrelenting play. These are likely dogs who were not properly socialized as puppies, and so never learned to "speak dog" very well. They never learned to read the language of another dog's "leave me alone" cues and will keep pushing until there's a fight. Hormones can also play a role, and that's why it's usually best for dog-park play to be among spayed and neutered animals.

Even if your dog is relaxed and comfortable in new situations and good with other dogs, you still have some work to do before heading to the park. Your dog must reliably come when called, so you can extricate him from an unsafe situation. If he won't come to you in your house, start teaching him by using voice commands and rewarding him with treats. Once he's reliable in the home, graduate to the backyard. Next, try somewhere safe and protected, like a friend's backyard, and add various distractions of other dogs and people around. Once you've reached this step, you're almost ready to head for the dog park.

Get the scoop on the local parks by going without your dog first. Find out the busiest part of the day (usually right after normal work hours and on weekends), the slowest (usually early mornings and midafternoons), and whether any aggressive dogs frequent the park. Visit at the time you'll usually be there, and observe what other dogs are regulars at that time. Your first concern is your dog's well-being and safety, and protecting him from any aggressive dogs who may visit the park is a must.

Look at the park's design, as well. Parks should have a double entry, a place you go in with your dog first to take off the leash and watch for the right moment to enter the main park—when there's not a huge crowd of dogs waiting to pounce on the newcomer. Since even well-meaning large dogs can hurt small dogs, it's best to find a park with a separate area for smaller dogs if you want to let your little guy run. You'll also want a park with good basic rules and an engaged group of users who enforce those rules—such as having all children under complete supervision of an adult (little kids can be easily injured by roughhousing dogs), a limit on the number of dogs a single person can bring in (no one can manage a dozen dogs at once), and, of course, a strict policy on immediate poop pick-ups.

If your dog is ready, and the park seems well managed, then it's time to try it out. Try taking your dog to the park at the least busy time of day at first. Letting your dog become adjusted to the surroundings with just a few dogs around him will help keep him from getting overwhelmed.

You may think that it's best to keep your dog on the leash at first, but in fact, off-leash is always better. When dogs are leashed, they have little freedom to play with other dogs that come up, and it's harder for them to get away from a dog they don't want to play with. So take off that leash!

Understand what kind of play is normal for different kinds of dogs. Herding dogs, for example, often prefer to chase other dogs and nip at their heels. Terriers tend to be more directly confrontational and may get into other dogs' faces and smash into them when playing. Depending on your dog's prior experiences, he may not be familiar with how other breeds play, so give him time to adapt. Keep dog-park sessions short, and leave at the earliest sign that your dog is getting anxious or overwhelmed.

Watch your dog at all times. It's poor dog-park etiquette—not to mention unsafe—to spend your time reading or talking to other dog owners while your dog is running unsupervised. Don't allow your dog to bully, or be bullied. Some people insist they have a right to use a dog park no matter how ill behaved or dangerous their dogs are around other dogs. When people like this come in, the best advice is to immediately head out with your dog and report the park user who is endangering others.

One of the best parts of using a dog park is getting to hang out with others who love dogs as much as you do. Since many dog parks are maintained, policed, and improved by those who use them, get active and join your dog park's association. It'll make going even more fun for you and your dog.

Melissa Bain, D.V.M., is a board-certified veterinary behaviorist and an assistant professor and chief of service of the Clinical Animal Behavior Service at the University of California, Davis, School of Veterinary Medicine. Her responsibilities include student and resident education, clinical case management, and research. Areas of research focus have been on clinical domestic animal behavior problems and human-animal bond issues, including research on dog parks and the effects of different training methods on the behavior of dogs. Dr. Bain is also an author of many articles and textbook chapters, as well as an invited speaker at many conferences. The University of California, Davis, School of Veterinary Medicine website is at www.vetmed.ucdavis.edu/small_animal/services/behavior.

Father and son retrievers share a moment, if not a ball.

The Brittany will happily hunt all day—whether for birds or tennis balls.

This dog knows the importance of staying hydrated.

A vizla pup surveying the landscape.

No matter what the weather, a dog is always ready to run.

If we were as enthusiastic about exercise as the average dog, we'd all be healthier.

Sitting and waiting isn't a dog's first choice, but she'll do it, for you.

Me? Digging?
Never!

Must-Know Info
Good Dog, Nice Yard?
Yes, It Is Possible!

---

*If you're a dog owner who dreams of a beautiful yard, take heart:
dogs and lush gardens aren't mutually exclusive.*

~ ~

But you can't just plant whatever you want where you want
and throw a bored, unsupervised dog into the mix. Instead, plan
your yard to take your dog into account, and mind your dog's
needs to get him to leave the plants alone. Here are the basic
guidelines:

Exercise your dog. A dog with too much energy is more likely
to engage in search-and-destroy missions, with your yard in her
sights. A dog who gets vigorous exercise on a daily basis will be
more likely to nap. Which would you rather have in your yard? In
addition to daily exercise, keep your dog busy with food or puzzle
toys when you can't be with her.

Supervise your dog. Don't leave your dog unattended in any
part of the yard you want left alone. Keep your dog in the house
when you can't supervise him (in just part of the house, if he's
destructive overall), or provide him with his own yard away from
the choicest parts of your property.

Work with your dog's habits. Observe how your dog uses your yard, and plan accordingly. For instance, many dogs consider it their duty to run the fence line, leaving a well-worn trail where many people hope to put flowers. Go with her natural instincts. Place your beds and plantings away from the fence line, and let her do her guard-dog patrolling behind those plants.

Redirect digging. Some breeds were developed to dig, and expecting them not to indulge in it is unfair. You can find most of these digging dogs in the terrier group—the word "terrier" comes from *terra*, for "earth." Put a dig zone in and praise your dog for using it. Make it the most enticing place to dig by burying treats for your dog to find. Limit access to dirt elsewhere, or supervise until your dog gets the idea.

Put special plants in safer places. Raised beds and hanging planters are the place to put your most precious plants. In areas where your dog will roam, put the plants that can take being stepped on in front. Ask your garden center for suggestions.

And what about the Number 1 thing people want fixed—yellow spots on the lawn? The easiest solution is to provide your dog with an out-of-sight "potty zone" and train her to use it. Take your dog directly to the potty patch and give a command, such as "Hurry up" or "Go potty." Praise for proper performance. Don't let your dog into the main part of the yard until she understands that her bathroom is around the corner.

If your dog does squat on the choicest patch of green, flush the area promptly with lots and lots of fresh water, which will dilute the urine and minimize its damaging effect.

What about products you can feed your dog that are supposed

to eliminate this problem? It's not a good idea to feed your dog anything that's not expressly for her benefit. One common recommendation of upping your dog's salt intake to encourage more water intake, causing urine dilution and thus a greener lawn, fails the common-sense test when it comes to your dog's health.

Cheryl S. Smith is an award-winning author, top dog trainer, and popular radio-show host who lives in the Pacific Northwest. Her book *Dog Friendly Gardens, Garden Friendly Dogs* earned rave reviews from dog trainers, gardening experts, and dog-loving gardeners. Her most recent book is *Grab Life by the Leash*. For more information visit her website, www.WriteDog.com.

Must-Know Info
Lost? . . .
and Found Quickly!

One of the biggest mistakes people make when pets go missing is underestimating the seriousness of the situation. When a pet gets out, the response should never be "wait and see." Your pet is about as capable of surviving on his own as a toddler is.

First on the to-do list: a "lost dog" sign.

Take a picture of your dog every year, so you'll have a current photograph to include on your sign. You don't need to describe your dog from nose to tail. If you've lost a large, black dog, start with that: "Lost! Large, black dog!"

Also put the word "reward" in big, clear letters. Money can be a powerful motivation for someone who doesn't care otherwise, and it can be an incentive for someone to tell you who has your pet if it was stolen.

Leave out a piece of information that only the true finder would know, such as a distinguishing mark or the color of your dog's collar. Asking the finder to describe your pet will thwart scam artists who prey on people with lost pets, claiming to have the pet to collect a reward.

Make sure the sign can be easily read from a distance of a

passerby walking or a car driving on the road. Include your phone number and area code—a cell phone number would be best (keep that phone with you and turned on).

A measure of "sappiness" should be your final touch: get people emotionally involved. Include "child is heartbroken" or "my best friend is missing." It really can help!

Print at least fifty signs on bright-colored paper and post them all around the area where your pet was lost. Post half of the signs so that they're facing the street where drivers can see them, and half facing the sidewalk, so pedestrians can read them. Poke a hole and thread a rubber band through the top of the flyer and hang copies from your neighbors' doorknobs. Post flyers in nearby places where the finder might go, such as veterinary offices, dog parks, pet-supply stores, groomers, grocery stores, and the post office.

If your dog has been microchipped, contact the registry to let them know your dog is missing.

Tell your mail carrier that your pet is missing, too!

Next, on your action list are these important tasks:

Place ads. Place a "lost dog" ad in local newspapers, and post it on Internet sites. Check the "found dog" ads in the same places.

Visit shelters. Visit every shelter within at least a fifty-mile radius of where your pet was lost. Since new pets are brought in daily, it's highly recommended that you go to the shelters every day. Shelter workers are busy, and they might not remember seeing your pet or recognize him from your verbal description, so visiting is better than calling. Ask to see the pets in the infirmary, as well as in the general runs, because your pet might have been injured. While you're at the shelters, ask to check the listings of animals who didn't make it, such as those hit by cars. Hard as it is to know a pet was killed, it's harder to never know what happened.

Change your phone message. Record a message on all your phones (home, office, cell) that encourages people to leave a message. Suggestion: "If you're calling about my missing pet, I'm out looking for him right now. Please leave a message, and I'll call you as soon as I come in."

Enlist help. Ask friends, family, and neighbors to help you search by going door-to-door in your area. Ask neighbors to check their garages, tool sheds, and crawl spaces. Small dogs often slip into such spaces unnoticed and are trapped when doors are shut behind them.

Just as you shouldn't delay in trying to find your pet, you shouldn't give up too easily. People may tell you you're nuts to keep looking, but pets do turn up after weeks and even months of searching. Make sure your signs stay posted and keep visiting the shelters.

Liz Blackman, inspired by her own two rescued dogs, Lita and Winchell, founded 1-800-HELP-4-PETS, an identification system that works like a nationwide 911 service for pets in any emergency—lost, home fire, car accident, natural disaster, and travel emergencies. Since 1996, 1-800-HELP-4-PETS has helped thousands of pets get help and get home. For more information, listings for lost and found pets, and advice on how to prevent loss or find a missing pet, visit these websites: www. help4pets.com and www.thecenterforlostpets.com.

Must-Know Info
K-911: Be Prepared for a Pet-Care Emergency

The old axiom, "the best way to treat an emergency is to prevent one" is true, especially when it comes to pets. In any emergency, dog lovers can misdiagnose or compound the problem if they don't have the proper information. Don't assume you know what's wrong with your dog. Instead, always err on the side of caution—call your veterinarian to find out if your pet needs to be seen right away.

There are some over-the-counter medications that are commonly used to treat dogs, and you should keep these on hand. They include aspirin, diphenhydramine (Benadryl), famotidine (Pepcid AC), ranitidine (Zantac), and dextromethorphan (Robitussin DM). Always check with your veterinarian to determine the dose and possible side effects before using these medications, since even the children's recommended dosage of these products can be more than a large dog can handle.

When is your dog's situation an emergency? You know your dog, and you know what her normal behavior and habits are. If something seems amiss—even if something "just doesn't feel right"—it is probably worth having a veterinarian check it out. Keep emergency numbers handy, and make sure anyone else looking after your pet has them on hand as well.

You have an emergency on your hands if your dog is showing any of the following symptoms:

- Difficulty breathing
- Straining to urinate
- Repeated vomiting
- Seizures
- Difficulty in giving birth
- Inability to get up
- Severe weakness or lethargy
- Not eating for more than 24 hours
- Bloody diarrhea
- Bleeding
- Pain

How do you know if your dog is in pain? Some dogs in pain will withdraw and not interact with their family, while others will readily show outward signs of pain by crying or being aggressive. The fact that pets can't tell us what hurts, how much it hurts, or how long it has been hurting further complicates the problem. Your dog is likely in pain if she is guarding or protecting a limb or other body part; is being less social, interactive, or playful; won't eat or lie down; or is constantly panting, whining, or crying.

Because an injured dog can further hurt herself or you, it's best to wrap the animal in a blanket (sometimes covering the eyes of a scared dog can help to calm her), place her on a flat, firm surface (such as in a sturdy box or on a piece of plywood) and head to the emergency clinic after notifying the staff that you are on the way, so they can be adequately prepared. Make sure that you are protected when you lift or move your injured dog—in a pinch, a pair of pantyhose can be fashioned into a muzzle that gently keeps your dog's mouth closed to prevent biting (although it's better to keep a muzzle on hand as part of your emergency kit).

Bleeding from skin injuries can usually be controlled with gentle pressure using a clean towel, a disposable diaper, or a feminine sanitary pad. Apply firm pressure for five minutes and then evaluate the area so see if bleeding has stopped. Avoid repeatedly peeking at the area, as you will disturb any blood clots that are trying to form. If you see spurting blood, apply constant pressure and head to the emergency clinic. An artery might be involved, and these usually require sedation or anesthesia and medical attention.

For any dog emergency, arrive at your vet's office or the clinic prepared to provide a good history. If you know your dog has gotten into household products, pesticides, or medication, bring the bottle or package with you. Know what medications your dog is on and any chronic health conditions she has.

And be patient: In the emergency clinic, pets are seen in the order of urgency. Your pet may need to wait to be treated if there's an animal there in a more life-threatening situation.

Above all, remember that your dog picks up on your emotions—so stay calm. Being prepared for an emergency will help you keep your cool.

Tony Johnson, D.V.M., is a board-certified veterinarian in veterinary emergency and critical care medicine. A former clinical assistant professor at Purdue University College of Veterinary Medicine, he currently is head of emergency services at Indiana Veterinary Specialists and Emergency Center in Indianapolis. Dr. Johnson is also a popular consultant for the Veterinary Information Network (http://veterinary partner.com). For more information visit www.indyvetspecialists.com.

> # Must-Know Info
> ## The Top Ten Household Hazards:
> ## Keeping Your Dog Safe

Some poisonings are a result of something an animal gets into, like a household product, but a surprising number of cases come from something the owner has intentionally given to an animal. A common example of the latter is when an elderly arthritic dog is given acetaminophen. The owner is trying to help, but unfortunately, even one capsule of this common human medicine can kill a dog.

At the ASPCA Animal Poison Control Center (APCC), we also see many cases where dogs chew, dig, or generally muscle their way into situations that their owners never envisioned. This includes opening cabinets to get cleaning products and "counter surfing" to reach food items and pill vials. Here's our rundown of reasons pet owners called in 2007, in order of the number of cases handled. Some represent serious concerns while others result from common, but not deadly, encounters:

1. Drugs meant for humans, both prescription and over-the-counter

2. Pesticides and herbicides, poisons meant to kill bugs, rodents, or weeds

3. Foods (chocolate accounted for about half of all food-related cases)

4. Biological hazards, primarily toxic plants (Lists of toxic plants can be found in pet reference books or on the ASPCA website)

5. Veterinary drugs

6. Cleaning products

7. Chemical hazards, such as acids, bases, alcohols, and gases

8. Metals, such as lead, zinc, mercury, and others

9. Cosmetics and personal care items, such as hair dye, hair relaxant or perms, and oral care or skin care products

10. General household hazards, such as batteries, matches, silica gel found in product packaging, ice melters, and air fresheners

And our not-so-honorable mention goes to home-improvement and hobby supplies, such as paint and adhesives.

Dog owners need to realize that their pets are like toddlers who can open most any childproof container and they must take similar precautions to protect them:

- Keep products such as medications, harmful foods, and cleaning products in a secure cabinet above countertop height.

- Use a kitchen garbage can with a secure lid.

- Always read labels, especially on flea and tick preparations and lawn and garden products. Store these out of reach in a high cupboard, not under the sink.

• Become familiar with the plants in and around your home, and keep only nontoxic plants in the house or any part of your yard your pet has access to.

• Never give any medication or nutritional supplement to your pet unless recommended or approved by your veterinarian.

There are many other toxic substances that aren't well known to dog owners. For example, don't let your dog have significant amounts of raisins or grapes, macadamia nuts, moldy cheese, chocolate, onions, garlic, or xylitol-sweetened gum, candies, or baked items.

Even with the best preventive measures in place, you need to know the signs of poisoning. Many (but not all) toxic substances will first cause stomach upset including vomiting and diarrhea. It's not fun, but vomit must be examined for evidence of chewed packaging, plant material, food, pills, or other clues to what your dog has ingested. Many poisonings can progress quickly to weakness and depression or to nervous stimulation including tremors and seizures. Pets may stop eating and drinking or may drink excessive amounts, which could suggest liver or kidney involvement. Rapid or slow breathing with changes in tongue and gum color, from pink to white, blue, or brown, indicate a critical situation that requires veterinary attention right away.

If your pet has gotten into something toxic, but isn't yet showing any symptoms, stay calm—panicking will not help your dog and may waste precious time. Contact your regular veterinarian or the ASPCA Animal Poison Control Center (1-888-426-4435) to determine if your pet needs to be seen or if treatment can be given at home.

If your dog is having difficulty breathing, is having seizures, is bleeding, or is unconscious, go to your regular veterinarian or emergency clinic immediately—you haven't time to spare if you're to save your pet's life. Take any evidence, including chewed containers and labels and even vomit. This information is key to helping your veterinarian save your pet.

Because you can't always get to an emergency clinic quickly, everyone should keep an emergency kit on hand. Your veterinarian or the APCC veterinarian may advise you to use these items immediately to save your dog's life. Here's what you need:

- A fresh bottle of hydrogen peroxide, 3 percent USP, to induce vomiting

- A turkey baster, bulb syringe, or large medicine syringe to administer hydrogen peroxide

- Saline eye solution for rinsing eyes

- Artificial tear gel to lubricate eyes after flushing

- Mild grease-cutting hand dishwashing liquid (such as Dawn, Ivory, or Palmolive) for bathing your dog after skin contamination

- Forceps to remove stingers and ticks (You can get these from many pet-supply retailers, especially those online or with mail-order service.)

- A muzzle to protect against fear- or excitement-induced biting

- A can of your dog's favorite wet food, to dilute any potential contaminant

Most important of all, be sure you always have the numbers of your pet's regular veterinarian, your local veterinary emergency clinic, and the ASPCA Animal Poison Control Center.

Steven Hansen, D.V.M., a board-certified specialist in toxicology and veterinary toxicology, is director of the ASPCA Animal Poison Control Center. He has authored several chapters in veterinary texts and has written peer-reviewed journal articles on the subject of animals and poison. Dr. Hansen is frequently consulted as a veterinary toxicology expert by the media and has appeared on countless news programs and in newspapers and magazines.

Dana Farbman, an Animal Poison Control Center's certified veterinary technician and head of professional communications, assisted on this article.

Must-Know Info
Anesthesia Is Safer
Than Ever for Pets

If there's one part of veterinary medicine that seems to worry the average dog owner most, it's anesthesia, especially when older pets are concerned.

⌒　⌒

The simplest definition of anesthesia is putting an animal into an unconscious state so the pet will be immobile and pain-free while a procedure is performed. Some dog owners consider anesthesia so high-risk that they refuse procedures that could have long-term benefits to a pet's health and comfort.

Although veterinary anesthesia can never be entirely risk-free, it's considerably safer and more comfortable now than ever. Veterinary medicine has benefited from the improved technology of human medicine: the same high-tech monitoring equipment is used to warn of problems with blood pressure, heart rhythm, and oxygenation. The safety margin is further increased with the addition of a qualified veterinary technician whose sole job is to watch those machines and to monitor the patient before, during, and after surgery.

While you might imagine veterinary anesthesia as a gas given through a mask over the animal's face, in fact the modern practice of preparing an animal for surgery is a no-size-fits-all combination of injectable medications (often combining anesthesia and pain-control agents), anesthesia-inducing gas, and pure oxygen, the latter two delivered through a breathing tube to maintain an animal's unconscious state.

In addition to constant monitoring by machines and trained technicians, the use of intravenous fluids during anesthesia is another safety measure. It gives the veterinarian instant access to a vein if there's an emergency. Intravenous fluids also help to prevent low blood pressure, which can be a common complication of most anesthetics.

Keeping an animal warm is another part of the safety protocols. A low body temperature delays anesthetic recovery and healing, and shivering increases oxygen consumption.

A pre-anesthetic screening is also important when it comes to reducing risk. A thorough physical exam allows the veterinarian to determine any underlying problems and to recommend pre-anesthetic blood work. In a young pet, that could be just checking for anemia. An older pet may need a complete blood count, determining kidney and liver function, and making sure all organs are functioning normally. Any abnormalities can be addressed before surgery to further increase safety margins.

Even in older pets, health problems don't necessarily rule out procedures that require general anesthesia. You have to balance the risks with the benefits; your veterinarian can discuss these with you. How much pain is the animal in? Has your pet stopped eating because of a rotting tooth? Many older pets have problems that dramatically reduce their quality of life and leave them in constant pain. Fear of anesthesia on the part of the owner is no reason to leave an animal in misery.

Not all veterinarians use all the anesthetic safety protocols— sometimes because of the cost concerns of pet owners. It's important to have a frank discussion with your veterinarian before your dog has surgery to understand how your pet will be treated and why. With a knowledge of what's available, you'll be able to make an informed decision when it comes to anesthesia and your pet.

Rachael Carpenter, D.V.M., is a clinical assistant professor of anesthesia and pain management at the University of Illinois College of Veterinary Medicine. She is also a consultant to the Veterinary Information Network. She has worked as an emergency and critical care veterinarian and did her internship at the prestigious Rood and Riddle Equine Hospital in Lexington, Kentucky.

Must-Know Info
Add Years to Your Dog's Life

Modern care and preventive measures can add years to your dog's life, but knowledge comes before action. And knowledge comes from developing a trusting, informed relationship with your veterinarian.

Your veterinarian can set up an appropriate program of preventive care for your dog, but frequent communication is important. Considering that animals age more quickly than we do, your veterinarian may suggest twice-yearly checkups, or even more frequent if your dog has health conditions that need to be closely monitored.

The more frequently your dog is checked, the more likely your veterinarian will be able to detect subtle changes and cues in your dog that may indicate potential health problems. Physical exams are also a time to conduct routine preventive care for your dog's ears, coat, nails, and teeth. During these wellness checks, your veterinarian can discuss other preventive care measures such as vaccinations and the control of parasites like fleas, ticks, and heartworm. Blood work and urinalysis should be conducted at least once a year by your vet. About 12 percent of patients with a healthy physical exam will show abnormalities on routine laboratory work. These tests can find early signs of problems of the dog's kidneys, liver, pancreas, and other vital internal organs.

Dental care is as important for dogs as it is for humans. Brushing your dog's teeth daily is recommended, using canine toothpastes that taste good to your pet. Regular cleanings and scalings by your vet will not only keep your pet "kissable" but will also prevent damage to internal organs caused by swallowing bacteria from infected gums and broken teeth.

Your veterinarian will also be able to advise you on home care that will keep your dog fit and trim. Just as in humans, extra weight on your dog damages the internal organs and can increase the likelihood of diseases like diabetes. Arthritis is another common consequence of excess weight. If you're free-feeding, stop. Break up your dog's daily food portions into smaller meals. And get your pet moving! For better health—and good behavior, too—your dog needs daily exercise, not just a long walk, but some real heart-pumping aerobic action. Talk to your veterinarian before starting any exercise program for an obese, out of shape, or elderly dog. And remember: Working out together is good for both you and your dog!

Keeping your dog happy and healthy for the longest possible lifespan isn't hard, but it does take some effort on your part. So call your veterinarian for that first snout-to-tail examination, and discuss what your dog needs to get his life on the right track.

Thomas Carpenter, D.V.M., is president of the American Animal Hospital Association and medical director of the Newport Harbor Animal Hospital in Costa Mesa, California.

Must-Know Info
Teaching Your Dog
Leash Manners

Despite an emphasis on good leash manners in training classes, many dog owners aren't motivated to practice polite walking enough to make it a habit for them and their dogs.

This is especially true in suburban and rural areas—where dogs have yards or acreage—as opposed to urban environments where a dog's only outlet for fresh-air exercise may be a walk on a leash. But all dogs should be taught good leash manners. Putting in the time needed to reinforce polite walking pays off handsomely in gaining a enjoyable walking companion.

When walking your dog, remember that the leash is not a steering wheel or handle. It's a safety belt, intended to prevent your dog from leaving. It's not to be used to pull him around, nor should he drag you along behind him. The leash should always be kept slack. If you keep it tight, your dog will think tension in the leash is normal.

To teach your dog to walk politely on a loose leash, start with your dog sitting by your left side. Hold the leash in your left hand and have a good supply of treats in your right hand. Make sure there's enough slack in the leash so that it stays loose when your dog is in the zone you've identified for polite walking—less than the length of a leash.

Use your "Let's walk!" cue in a cheerful tone of voice and start walking forward. The instant your dog begins to move forward with you, use an audible "marker," such as the word, "Yes!" and give your dog a treat. (The "Yes!" is used to "mark" the behavior you want the dog to repeat, and the treat reinforces that behavior.)

"Yes!" and treat very frequently in the beginning, with almost every step. "Yes!" and treat as long as there's no tension in the leash, and the dog stays on your left side so that you don't trip over him. When your dog realizes it's worthwhile to stay within the designated area of his generous, treat-dispensing machine (you!), you can gradually reduce the rate of reinforcement—fewer "Yes!" markers and treats.

The manner in which you hold and deliver your treats is critical to success with polite walking. When you walk, keep your treat hand hidden behind your hip on the side opposite your dog. If you hold the treats on the same side where your dog can see or smell them, it will be harder to "fade" (slowly eliminate) the presence of the treats later on. If you hold them in front of you, your dog will likely keep stepping in front of you to watch your hand with the treats.

To deliver treats, wait for a second after the "Yes!" as you keep walking, then bring your hand across the front of your body, and feed the treat. Quickly move your hand back behind your hip as soon as you've delivered the treat. Feeding the treat in the location where you want your dog to be reinforces that position.

Direction changes can be useful in teaching polite leash walking. When your dog starts to move ahead of you, before he gets to the end of his leash, turn around and walk in the opposite direction.

Do this gently; you don't want him to hit the end of the leash with a jerk if he doesn't turn with you! As you turn, use your cheerful voice and a kissy noise to let him know you've changed direction.

When he notices and turns to come with you, say "Yes!" and offer a treat. He's now behind you, and you'll have lots of opportunities to say "Yes!" and provide a treat while he's in the loose-leash zone as he catches up and walks with you.

There will be times when your dog pulls ahead of you on a tight leash. This is a great opportunity to play "Be a tree." When the leash tightens, stop walking. Just stand still—like a tree—and wait, no cues or verbal corrections. Be sure to hug your leash arm to your side, so he can't pull you forward.

Eventually, your dog will wonder why his forward progress has stopped and will look back at you to see why you're not coming. When he does, the leash will slacken. In that instant, say "Yes!" and offer him a treat at your side. The "Yes!" marks the loose-leash behavior; he'll have to return to the reinforcement zone to get the treat. Then move forward until he's walking politely with you again.

Although they don't teach your dog to walk politely, there are some notable training tools that can help you control your pet and allow you to take him out without having your arm pulled from your shoulder. The head halter and the front-clip harness have become popular in recent years because they provide dog owners with a degree of control without harming the dog through the use of harsher methods frowned on by many trainers and behaviorists.

Still, it's good to remember that these are control tools, not training tools, and it's better to take the time to teach your dog to walk politely on a loose leash.

If you're having problems teaching your dog polite walking, if your frustration is growing to the point that your dog almost never leaves home, get some help! Find a trainer or behaviorist who can offer you advice and assistance on the tools and techniques you need to get you over the roadblock and back on the road.

Pat Miller is a certified dog behavior consultant, certified pet dog trainer, and past president of the Association of Pet Dog Trainers. Miller offers group good manners classes, private training and behavior modification services, dog training camps/clinics, and trainer academies at her Peaceable Paws eighty-acre training facility in Fairplay, Maryland, where she lives with her husband, Paul, and their four dogs, three cats, and many horses. In addition, Miller presents seminars and workshops around the world on a variety of training and behavior topics. She has authored four books: *The Power of Positive Dog Training, Positive Perspectives, Positive Perspectives 2,* and *Play with Your Dog.* Miller is training editor for the *Whole Dog Journal* and also writes for *Bark* magazine, Tufts University's *Your Dog,* and several other publications.

Must-Know Info
Meet and Greet: Socializing Is the Key to a Great Canine Companion

The first three months of a dog's life are critical, although this is something too few people understand. There is a true urgency to socializing a puppy, and opportunities missed by the age of thirteen weeks can never be fully recovered. Puppies are often introduced to new dogs and new people for the first time when they enter puppy class, typically starting at twelve weeks, but by that time much of who they are, and will be, has already been settled.

Most puppies are adopted at eight weeks of age. By that age, two-thirds of the most critical socialization period is already behind them. When considering a puppy, be sure you're dealing with a source—shelter or breeder—that has taken the time to intentionally introduce new sights, sounds, smells, and lots of gentle handing by a variety of people into the lives of the puppies. Many times, you can count on one hand the number of people a puppy has met before it is adopted at eight weeks. A puppy should meet as many people of all kinds—young and old, male and female—as possible. Considering that boys, who are often more active and aggressive than girls, are the most frequently bitten, often while teasing or frightening dogs, it's important that young puppies be exposed to as many boys as possible.

If a puppy shows any sign of fear around people, choose another puppy. A puppy who isn't outgoing and friendly will most likely be forever standoffish and afraid. Before you decide to bring a puppy home, watch how it reacts to all kinds of people, particularly men and children.

Once you have picked up your puppy at eight weeks, you still have five weeks left of the critical socialization period. Ideally, your puppy should meet one hundred new people in this period. If the puppy sees only family for the first months of its life, he or she will develop a fear of strangers.

To avoid this, invite different people into your home each week during the first three months of your puppy's life. Invite people over for dinner or to watch TV, and have children over to play. What matters is that the puppy is held, fed, and played with by as many new people as possible.

Save food from your puppy's regular meals so that visitors can feed your puppy by hand. This helps reinforce the idea that new people are wonderful. Have your visitors hug and handle the dog as much as possible, every square inch from nose to toes to tail. Make sure all visitors, especially children, are handling your puppy gently and with respect, that they don't drop the puppy or cause fear. Since children may not be strong enough to hold a wriggling puppy in their arms, have them sit cross-legged on the floor with the puppy in their lap.

Taking your puppy on walks is another way to meet new people.

Take along treats, and when you meet people, ask them to feed and pet your puppy. This continues to reinforce the idea that new people are friendly and will offer treats and attention. Getting a puppy out and about is especially important for people who live alone, because they often have fewer chances to meet other people. Go to places where people congregate, such as family gatherings or outdoor patios at coffeehouses. Visiting dog parks or other places frequented by high numbers of animals of questionable health status is not a good idea until the puppy has been fully vaccinated, but exposure to known friendly, healthy dogs is important.

Along with socializing, you need to teach your puppy to use his teeth properly. Learning not to bite hard—behaviorists call this "bite inhibition"—is important because, if a dog does bite, that inhibited nip will not cause damage.

Puppy class is a great way for a puppy to learn bite inhibition. In puppy class, puppies can play-fight with other puppies, learning that a hard bite hurts. This teaches puppies to be careful with their teeth and develop a gentle bite. You can also do the same thing by yelling a dramatic "ouch!" if your puppy nips too hard, and ending the play session, so the youngster learns that nipping ends the fun.

Although this early training is important for all dogs, it's especially important for those breeds known for being standoffish or preferring to bond with a single person. For example, chows and many other Asian breeds are standoffish, and German shepherds tend to form a close bond with only one person. If you have a puppy from one of these breeds, you need to work even more to socialize it properly. The more positive handling and experiences with people these puppies can get, the friendlier they become.

No matter what breed or type of dog you choose, don't let your puppy grow up without the lessons that will set the stage for a lifetime of friendliness and good manners.

Ian Dunbar, Ph.D., B.V.M., is a veterinarian and animal behaviorist who created and taught the world's first off-leash puppy socialization classes. He has written numerous books, including *How to Teach a New Dog Old Tricks* and *Doctor Dunbar's Good Little Dog Book*, and has hosted eleven DVDs on puppy and dog behavior and training, including *SIRIUS Puppy Training*. Dr. Dunbar is the founder of the Association of Pet Dog Trainers (www.apdt.com). His website is at www.dogstardaily.com.

Must-Know Info
The Perfect Puppy Pedicure
The Ultimate Coauthors

There are few things both people and dogs like less than clipping a dog's nails. There is an easier way: grind your dog's nails.

⌒   ⌒

Many professional groomers and in-the-know dog owners now grind nails with few complaints from their canine charges. If you buy a grinder made especially for dogs, it'll come with the correct grinding head. Otherwise, choose a medium grit sandpaper or stone tip for a standard hobby grinder, such as the Dremel.

Initially, just let your dog see the grinder, then praise and treat. In a later session, turn the grinder on and praise and treat. Continue to praise and treat, allowing the grinder to get closer to a paw and to briefly touch a nail tip. The first time you actually grind, be happy with working a little with just one nail, and don't forget to praise and treat.

You will need to either clip the hair of long-haired dogs or hold it back, so it won't get wound in the shaft of the grinder. Support the dog's toe, but don't squeeze too hard. Hold the grinder against the nail for no more than a couple of seconds at a time to prevent heat buildup, and don't push the grinder against the nail—let the grinder do the work.

Grind across the bottom edge of the nail and then carefully in from the tip of the nail. Just a little bit at a time is plenty. If you do this weekly, the quick will recede, and you'll be able to maintain short nails on your dog with ease.

Must-Know Info
Oooh, That's Bad:
Doing Away With "Doggy Breath"
The Ultimate Coauthors

---

*Controlling mouth odors is both an aesthetic and a health issue.
Dental cleanings are an important part of preventive medicine, and
keeping teeth clean between veterinary appointments is something that
can—and should—be done by dog owners.*

Plaque buildup on teeth causes gums to recede, opening pockets at the root line that are a paradise to bacterial infections. Left
unchecked, such infections can lead to tooth loss, make eating
painful, and stress the dog's immune system and internal organs
causing illness and premature aging. Rotting teeth and infected
gums are often the source of "doggy breath" that some pet owners treat with products that may temporarily fix the smell, but do
nothing about the real problem.

While some groomers and dog owners scale plaque themselves,
this doesn't address the problem at the root line and in fact may
make the problem worse (and provide a false sense of security for
the owner), so regular cleanings under anesthesia by a veterinarian are essential to ensure dental health. In between, attention

two or three times a week—daily is even better—with a toothbrush and a toothpaste designed for dogs slows the reformation of plaque and extends the time between full dental cleanings at the veterinarian's.

Getting a pet used to having his teeth brushed is best done by approaching it in small steps over time, being patient and encouraging. The toothpastes designed for dogs (who can't rinse, after all, so they're made to be swallowed) have flavors dogs dig, so that certainly helps.

Resources

American Animal Hospital Association (AAHA), 12575 W. Bayaud Avenue, Lakewood, CO 80228; Phone: 1-800-252-2242; website: www.healthypet.com

Established in 1933, the American Animal Hospital Association is the only organization that accredits veterinary practices throughout the United States and Canada for dedication to high standards of veterinary care. More than three thousand AAHA-accredited practices pass regular reviews of AAHA's stringent accreditation standards that cover patient care, client service, and medical protocols. Contact AAHA for pet-care information or referral to an AAHA-accredited practice.

American Society for the Prevention of Cruelty to Animals (ASPCA), 424 E. 92nd Street, New York, NY 10128; Phone: 212-876-7700; website: www.aspca.org

Founded in 1866, the ASPCA aims to prevent cruelty and alleviate the pain, fear, and suffering of animals by providing local and national programs that assist thousands of animals nationwide. The ASPCA's national programs include the Animal Poison Control Center, humane education, companion animal services, and national shelter outreach.

American Veterinary Medical Association (AVMA), 1931 North Meacham Road, Suite 100, Schaumburg, IL 60173; Phone: 847-925-8070; website: www.avma.org

The AVMA, founded in 1863, is one of the oldest and largest veterinary medical organizations in the world. Its more than seventy-six thousand member veterinarians recognize the importance of the human-animal bond and the veterinarian's role in preserving, protecting, and strengthening relationships between people and animals. AVMA members contribute to the health and well-being of animals through their work in clinical practice, public health, regulatory agencies, the uniformed services, and research.

American Kennel Club (AKC), 5580 Centerview Drive, Raleigh, NC 27606; Phone: 919-233-9767; website: www.akc.org

Founded in 1884, the AKC is a not-for-profit organization that maintains the largest registry of purebred dogs in the world and oversees the sport of purebred dogs in the United States. More than twenty thousand competitions for AKC-registered purebred dogs are held under AKC rules and regulations each year including conformation, agility, and obedience. Along with its nearly five thousand licensed and member clubs and affiliated organizations, the AKC advocates for the purebred dog as a family companion, advances canine health and well-being, works to protect the rights of all dog owners, and promotes responsible dog ownership.

AKC Canine Health Foundation (AKCCHF), 5580 Centerview Drive, Raleigh, NC 27606; Phone: 1-888-682-9696; website: www.akcchf.org

Founded in 1995, the **American Kennel Club Canine Health Foundation** is the largest not-for-profit funder of exclusively canine research in the world. The foundation works to develop significant resources for basic and applied health programs with emphasis on canine genetics to improve the quality of life for dogs and their owners. The foundation funds research and supports canine health scientists and professionals in their efforts to study the causes and origins of canine disease and afflictions to formulate effective treatments.

Animal Behavior Resources Institute (ABRI), P.O. Box 27348, Golden Valley, MN 55427; Phone: 612-209-1578; website: www.ABRIonline.org

ABRIonline.org provides free training and behavior resources to companion animal professionals and their clients. Resources include videos, podcasts, interviews, articles, and research studies featuring leading veterinarians, behaviorists, trainers, and other professionals. The ABRI's mission is to enhance human-animal relationships and improve quality of life for people and animals by providing high-quality education and animal behavior information.

Delta Society, 875 124th Avenue NE, Suite 101, Bellevue, WA 98005; Phone: 425-679-5500; website: www.deltasociety.org

Delta Society's mission is to improve human health through service and therapy animals. The organization works to expand awareness of the positive effects animals can have on human health, reduce barriers that prevent the involvement of animals in everyday life, and expand the therapeutic and service role of animals in human health, service, and education. Delta Pet Partners volunteers visit hospitals, nursing homes, schools, hospices, and other facilities with their pets providing animal-assisted activities and therapy throughout the United States and the world. The Pet Partners Program registers all types of pets including dogs, cats, rabbits, birds, horses, and other domestic animals.

The Humane Society of the United States (HSUS), 2100 L Street NW, Washington, DC 20037; Phone: 202-452-1100; website: www.humanesociety.org

The HSUS is the nation's largest animal protection organization, and it supports building and enhancing the human–companion animal bond through its Pets for Life campaign. Pets for Life provides solutions to behavior issues, restrictions on rental housing, and the concerns of allergic, pregnant, or immune-compromised individuals and promotes humane animal care and adoption to end the relinquishment, abandonment, and euthanasia of healthy dogs and cats.

Morris Animal Foundation (MAF), 10200 East Girard Avenue, Suite B430, Denver, CO 80231; Phone: 1-800-243-2345; website: www.MorrisAnimalFoundation.org

Established in 1948, the MAF is dedicated to funding research that protects, treats, and cures companion animals and wildlife. MAF has been at the forefront of funding breakthrough research studies benefiting animals in some one hundred countries, spanning all seven continents. With its headquarters in Denver, Colorado, the Foundation has funded nearly fourteen hundred humane animal health studies with funds totaling more than $51 million.

PetConnection.com, website: www.PetConnection.com

The online home of Marty Becker, D.V.M., "America's Veterinarian," and his writing partner, Gina Spadafori. The two are syndicated columnists and top-selling pet-care authors. Together with other members of the PetConnection.com team, they offer pet lovers a free, searchable library of top-quality pet medical and behavior advice, as well as other resources, including newsletters and contests. The Pet Connection.com blog is the pet lover's must-go daily check-in for the latest in pet health and animal advocacy news. PetConnection.com's affiliated site, DogCars.com, offers free reviews of new vehicles and travel advice for dog lovers.

The Writers

Christine Albers lives in Fairfield, Iowa, and works as a sales manager. Her passion is writing short stories, and she has published several in magazines and literary journals. She enjoys her Monday night writing group, yoga, daily Transcendental Meditation, cooking vegetarian meals, and long walks in the park with her dog, Bud.

Marianne Allen was born and raised in Sweden and moved to the United States in 1981. Marianne is a freelance massage therapist in Southern California. Marianne and her partner, Robert, have always shared their home with two to three dogs at a time, adopted from the pound, animal shelter, or rescued off the street.

Melissa Bain, D.V.M., is a board-certified veterinary behaviorist, and an assistant professor and chief of service of the Clinical Animal Behavior Service at the University of California, Davis, School of Veterinary Medicine. Her responsibilities include student and resident education, clinical case management, and research. Areas of research focus have been on clinical domestic animal behavior problems and human-animal bond issues, including research on dog parks and the effects of different training methods on the behavior of dogs. Dr. Bain is also an author of many articles and textbook chapters, as well as an invited speaker at many conferences. The University of California, Davis, Veterinary Medicine website is www.vetmed.ucdavis.edu/small_animal/services/behavior.

D. Lynn Black has contributed to a variety of publications including *Country Woman*, *Hobby Farms*, and *American Profile Magazine*. She also raises show-quality Nigerian Dwarf goats under her Moon Spinner herd in western New York. An avid nature lover, Lynn enjoys hiking in the company of her beloved dogs. Please visit her website www.angelfire.com/moon2/moonspinner.

Liz Blackman was inspired by her own two rescued dogs, Lita and Winchell, and founded 1-800-HELP-4-PETS, an identification system that works like a nationwide 911 service for pets in any emergency—lost, home fire, car accident, natural disaster, and travel emergencies. Since 1996, 1-800-HELP-4-PETS has helped thousands of pets get help and get home. For more information, listings for lost and found pets, and advice on how to prevent loss or find a missing pet, visit these websites: www.help4pets.com and www.thecenterforlostpets.com.

Deborah Blair is a graduate of Loyola Marymount University. Her articles have been published in *Music Technology*, *Rhythm*, *Electronic Musician*, and *Home & Studio Recording*. She currently shares her home with a bevy of beautiful golden retrievers.

Harris Bloom is a writer, stand-up comic, dog lover, and zombie (he played one in a movie). Stewie and Harris have appeared on the CBS *Early Show* to test a pet IQ test. Harris also produces and hosts an annual benefit comedy show for Canines Unleashed, his local dog run, and can be reached at http://www.myspace.com/harrisbloom.

Amanda Borozinski is a full-time reporter and photographer for the *Keene Sentinel*, a daily newspaper in Keene, New Hampshire. Her work has appeared in *Guideposts* magazine, *Positive Thinking* magazine, TheHorse.com, the *Northern New England Review*, the *Oklahoma Review*, and the *Boston Globe*. In 2008, she was awarded a fellowship from the prestigious MacDowell Colony and spent three secluded weeks working on an upcoming book project. Amanda can be reached at aboro@ptcnli.net.

Marcia E. Brown, an Austin, Texas, widow, has been sharing her family stories in print for the past fifteen years. She has been widely published in magazines, newspapers, and anthologies, including two previous Chicken Soup for the Soul collections. Several of her stories have won awards. As a freelancer, she also writes articles and poetry. You can reach Marcia by e-mail at Wordeze@yahoo.com.

Isabel Bearman Bucher and her husband, Robert, continue their honeymoon with life. In January 2008, they adopted a little dog, Maisie, from the Animal Humane Society; their first dog in over twenty-five years and enjoy their eldest daughter's three adopted stray cats. Isabel began yet another adventure, developing a website where her first book, *Nonno's Monkey, an Italian American Memoir*, can be found. She's made it a home to begin geneology searches, how-to write a family recipe book, travel info, and more. Many stories from the memoir can be found in past Chicken Soup for the Soul anthologies. Enjoy her work on the Web at isabelbucher.com; isabelbearmanbucher.com, and oneitaliana.com.

Rachael Carpenter, D.V.M., is a clinical assistant professor of anesthesia and pain management at the University of Illinois College of Veterinary Medicine. She is also a consultant to the Veterinary Information Network. She has worked as an emergency and critical care veterinarian and did her internship at the prestigious Rood and Riddle Equine Hospital in Lexington, Kentucky.

Thomas Carpenter, D.V.M., is president of the American Animal Hospital Association and medical director of the Newport Harbor Animal Hospital in Costa Mesa, California.

Diane M. Ciarloni lives in Texas with a houseful of dogs, cats, rabbits, and birds and a barn full of horses. She is a professional freelance writer with work appearing in several national anthologies. Diane is also the author of *Legends*, a special-interest book about horses. You can contact Diane by e-mail at eaglesrest@centurytel.net.

J. Vincent Dugas, now a semiretired business owner, is dusting off hundreds of stories he wrote during his life for his own amusement.

Ian Dunbar, Ph.D., B.V.M., is a veterinarian and animal behaviorist who created and taught the world's first off-leash puppy socialization and training classes. He has written numerous books, including *How to Teach a New Dog Old Tricks* and the *Good Little Dog Book*, and has hosted eleven DVDs on puppy and dog behavior and training, including *SIRIUS Puppy Training*. Dr. Dunbar is the founder of the Association of Pet Dog Trainers (www.apdt.com). His website is www.dogstardaily.com.

Aubrey H. Fine, Ed.D., is the editor of the most widely accepted book on animal assisted therapy (AAT), *The Handbook on Animal Assisted Therapy*, which is now in its second edition (Elsevier/Academic Press, 2006). Dr. Fine writes a featured monthly column in *Dog Fancy* magazine entitled "Loving Bond," and his newest book, *Afternoons with Puppy* (Purdue University, 2008, www.afternoonswithpuppy.com), is a heartwarming account of the evolving relationships and outcomes experienced by a therapist, his therapy animals, and his patients over the course of two decades.

Peggy Frezon is the winner of the 2004 *Guideposts* writer's contest and the *Children's Writer* personal story contest in 2007. Publishing credits include *Guideposts*, *Teaching Tolerance*, *Positive Thinking*, *Pockets*, *Miracles and Animals*, Chicken Soup for the Soul, and others. She's presently working on a book about weight loss for dogs. Please visit her blog, "The Writer's Dog" at http://thewritersdog.blogspot.com.

Maria Goodavage is author of the popular thousand-page guidebook, *The Dog Lover's Companion to California*, and two other books in the Dog Lover's Companion series. Maria, a former *USA Today* reporter, is chauffeur to her research assistant, Jake, a yellow Labrador who has no driver's license—yet. They live near a dog-friendly beach in San Francisco with Maria's husband and daughter. Find out more about Maria and Jake's books at www.caldogtravel.com.

Craig Griffin, D.V.M., is a diplomate of the American College of Veterinary Dermatology and the founder and co-owner of the Animal Dermatology Clinic. He is a frequent lecturer and clinical instructor of veterinary dermatology, and he has published many articles and books on small animal skin disease. Dr. Griffin has received the ACVD Award for Excellence for outstanding contributions in veterinary dermatology. The Animal Dermatology Clinic has four permanent locations: Tustin, San Diego, and Marina del Rey, California; and Marietta, Georgia. There are also eleven satellite clinics. The website for Animal Dermatology Clinic and Dr. Craig Griffin is www.animaldermatology.com.

Lila Guzman writes children's fiction and nonfiction. Her latest novel, *Kichi in Jungle Jeopardy* (Blooming Tree Press), is about a Chihuahua in ancient Mayan times. Visit Lila at www.lilaguzman.com.

Rachael HaileSelasse grew up in Wyoming and traveled throughout North America and Africa for several years before earning a B.A. in international/African studies from the University of Oregon. While working in Ethiopia, Rachael met and married Mesfin. Lucky's rescue is only a portion of the adventures that the young couple lived in east Africa. Rachael returned to the United States, bringing Lucky with her. They have made their home together in the state of Washington and await the immigration of Mesfin.

Steven Hansen, D.V.M., a board-certified specialist in toxicology and veterinary toxicology, is director of the ASPCA Animal Poison Control Center. He has authored several chapters in veterinary texts and has written peer-reviewed journal articles on the subject of animals and poison. Dr. Hansen is frequently consulted as a veterinary toxicology expert by the media and has appeared on countless news programs and in newspapers and magazines. **Dana Farbman** is an Animal Poison Control Center certified veterinary technician and head of professional communications.

Tony Johnson, D.V.M., is a board-certified veterinarian in veterinary emergency and critical care medicine. A former clinical assistant professor at Purdue University College of Veterinary Medicine, he currently is head of emergency services at Indiana Veterinary Specialists and Emergency Center in Indianapolis. Dr. Johnson is also a popular consultant for the Veterinary Information Network (http://veterinarypartner. com). For more information visit www.indyvetspecialists.com.

Mimi Greenwood Knight is a freelance writer living in southern Louisiana with her husband, David, children Haley, Molly, Hewson, and Jonah, and a delightful menagerie of pets. Her work has appeared in *Parents*, *Working Mother*, *American Baby*, *Living Magazine*, *Today's Christian Woman*, *In Touch*, *HomeLife*, *At-Home Mother*, *Christian Parenting Today*, *Sesame Street Parents*, and a smattering of anthologies.

Liisa Kyle raises Guide Dog puppies in addition to her work as an editor, writing coach, and prize-winning, internationally published writer/photographer. As a consultant specializing in creativity, communication, and organization, she has coached individuals, facilitated groups, and delivered inventive workshops on four continents. To learn more about her recent book, please visit www.liisakyle.com.

Gary Landsberg, D.V.M., is board-certified in veterinary behavior both in North America and in Europe. In addition to his general veterinary practice, Dr. Landsberg offers behavior consultation services at the North Toronto Animal Clinic. He is a frequent speaker on behavioral topics at veterinary conferences around the world and has coauthored a number of veterinary behavioral texts as well as a series of behavior brochures. Dr. Landsberg has also hosted his own TV and radio shows. He was awarded the American Animal Hospital Association award for his contributions to the field of companion animal behavior and is a past president of the American College of Veterinary Behaviorists. His website is www.northtorontovets.com.

Linda Mehus-Barber lives with her loving husband, affectionately known as the Buffalo, and their two dogs and cat in the seaside community of Crescent Beach in Surrey, British Columbia. When Linda is not teaching or writing, she loves to hike in the mountains or walk along the beach with her husband and dogs.

Jacki Michels has eighteen chickens, five children, four grandchildren, one dog (as Terra recently passed away), one goldfish, and one well housebroken husband—all of whom she loves dearly. She is a regular humor and news columnist for the *Peninsula Clarion* in Kenai Alaska. You may contact her at jackimichels@hotmail.com.

Pat Miller is a certified dog behavior consultant, certified pet dog trainer, and past president of the Association of Pet Dog Trainers. Miller offers group good manners classes, private training and behavior modification services, dog training camps/clinics, and trainer academies at her Peaceable Paws eighty-acre training facility in Fairplay, Maryland, where she lives with her husband, Paul, and their four dogs, three cats, and many horses. In addition, Miller presents seminars and workshops around the world on a variety of training and behavior topics. She has authored four books: *The Power of Positive Dog Training*, *Positive Perspectives*, *Positive Perspectives 2*, and *Play with Your Dog*. Miller is training editor for the *Whole Dog Journal* and also writes for *Bark* magazine, Tufts University's *Your Dog*, and several other publications.

Bill Mullis writes in the South Carolina Upstate, surrounded by his family, some human, some furry. Bo has him trained to drive the car on the weekly trip to the dump.

Linda Newton and her husband, Bruce, live in the California foothills. Their kids are grown, making room for two dogs and one cat—including Gus, the angel dog. You will find other stories by Linda in *Chicken Soup for the Chocolate Lover's Soul*. She recently published her first book, *Twelve Ways to Turn Your Pain into Praise*. Visit Linda at www.lindanewtonspeaks.com.

Gregory Ogilvie, D.V.M., is director of the Angel Care Cancer Center at California Veterinary Specialists and president of the Special Care Foundation for Companion Animals where he continues to care for patients and their families, teach interns, residents, and veterinary students, and leads an active cancer research program. Prior to his move to Southern California, Dr. Ogilvie was a full tenured professor, internist, head of medical oncology, and director of the medical oncology research laboratory Animal Cancer Center at Colorado State University from 1987 until 2003. Dr. Ogilvie lectures to thousands of aspiring and graduate veterinarians and scientists each year and has been recognized as Veterinarian of the Year by both the American Veterinary Medical Association and the American Animal Hospital Association, among many other awards.

Pierre O'Rourke worked as an artist, firefighter, celebrity interviewer, maître d', columnist, publicist, and author media guide—while he tried to figure out what to be when he grew up. Bestselling authors and prominent celebrities with whom he had worked over the years urged him to begin writing books. It only took him eleven years to listen and take action. He writes in Scottsdale, Arizona, with his furry pal Nubble. Neither has plans of growing up anytime soon. You can reach Pierre at pierrewrites@cox.net.

Liz Palika has been training dogs and their owners for more than twenty-five years in Southern California. She is a certified dog trainer, behavioral consultant, and an American Kennel Club Canine Good Citizen evaluator. Liz is also an award-winning author who has written more than fifty books on pets, including *The Complete Idiot's Guide to Dog Tricks* (2005). Her newest book is *The Howell Book of Dogs* (2007). For more information, visit www.lizpalika.com.

Carrie Pepper, a freelance writer based in Sacramento, California, has written on a variety of topics, including health/sports, environmental issues and natural resources, for local and national publications. She is currently working on a collection of short stories (many of which are animal-related) titled *The Nose in the Knothole and Other Stories*, as well as a memoir related to herbrother's death in Vietnam. She has rescued, and written about, cats, dogs, rabbits —and most recently, a California gull. You can read more about Carrie at www.carriepepper.com.

Lisa Price is a freelance writer living in Pennsylvania with four dogs—three German shorthaired pointers (Josey Wales, Lozen, and Prairie) and a black terrier mix (Bama, rescued from the side of the road in Alabama). Lisa's first word was "bowwow."

Carol McAdoo Rehme directs Vintage Voices, Inc., a nonprofit providing interactive programs for Northern Colorado long-term care facilities. Jazzy, eleven and still "Matriarch of the Manor," goes where everybody knows her name. Carol publishes widely in the inspirational market. She is the coauthor of *Chicken Soup for the Empty Nester's Soul* (2008).

Calder Reid works for the U.S. Forest Service as a wilderness coordinator. She spent many years as a seasonal wilderness ranger patrolling the John Muir Wilderness. Dogs have always been a part of Calder's life. When she was young she volunteered at the SPCA and went to dog shows with her mother who is a Pembroke Welsh corgi breeder and AKC judge.

Kimberly Ripley is a freelance writer and published author from New Hampshire. A wife and mother of five, she writes with her faithful dog, Philly, at her feet.

Teresa Rodney lives in Fountain Valley, California, with her husband and three dogs (an eleven-and-half-year-old Australian shepherd named Smokey, a nine-year-old flat-coated retriever named Jazz, and a three-year-old flat-coat named Sprint). Teresa competes with all three dogs in a variety of events such as conformation, obedience, and hunt tests but concentrates on agility, which she loves. She has been competing in agility since 1995. As of the publishing of this book, Jazz just celebrated her ninth birthday. She is thriving and still running agility sixteen months after her diagnosis of malignant cancer, in which she was given only six to eight months to live.

Sheri Ryan is the married mother of three. She is employed as an administrative assistant and also does freelance copywriting and editing. Sheri enjoys spending time with family and friends, and her dream is to write a bestselling novel and screenplay. You can contact Sheri by e-mail at sryan@intergrafix.net.

Betty Sleep is a freelance writer and author of the award-winning children's book *Purrlock Holmes and the Case of the Vanishing Valuables*. She and Leah live in New Brunswick, Canada, with another rescued golden retriever and an assortment of Birman cats.

Cheryl S. Smith is an award-winning author, top dog trainer, and popular radio-show host who lives in the Pacific Northwest. Her book *Dog Friendly Gardens, Garden Friendly Dogs* earned rave reviews from dog trainers, gardening experts, and dog-loving gardeners. Her most recent book is *Grab Life by the Leash*. For more information visit her website, www.WriteDog.com.

Traci R. Smith resides in a rural Kansas town with her wonderful husband, two beautiful children, two spoiled hound dogs, and one pampered cat. Formerly a nursing home social worker, Traci now spends her days caring for her children and weaving her experiences with the many people who have enriched her life into the tapestry of her freelance writing. She welcomes contact at btd.smith@sbcglobal.net.

Troy Snow is a professional freelance photographer whose work has been widely appreciated and published. Along with a team from Best Friends, he went to the Gulf Coast in the aftermath of Hurricane Katrina to help animals and people. The stories from that rescue effort are told by his stunning photos in the book *Not Left Behind: Rescuing the Pets of New Orleans*. Many of Snow's photographs can be found on the Best Friends website (www.bestfriends.org) and you can see more of his work at www.troysnowphoto.com.

Bonnie West has been previously published in *Chicken Soup for the Woman's Soul* and *Chicken Soup for the Shopper's Soul*. She has produced a CD, *Yoga for Writers*, and can be reached at yogabonnie@yahoo.com. She is working on a novel; watch for it!

Jon Wong, a periodontist and recovering large-caninophile, now wants to raise large packs of free-range miniature schnauzers. He and girlfriend Jan (a general dentist who takes very good care of her dogs) were heartbroken when Franny, the sweetest dog on earth, recently lost her battle with kidney failure. Their other dog, Daisy, was stricken with SARD four months after her sister but is doing well. Jan, Jon, and Daisy live in Ojai, California.

Dallas Woodburn is the author of two short story collections and numerous articles for magazines including *Family Circle* and *Writer's Digest*. You can reach Dallas through her website, www.zest.net/writeon.

The Photographers

Rita Kay Adams's passion is, and always has been, animals and photography. Through the years Rita has had many cats and dogs, each special, each endearing. Her Dobie, Voodoo (Marienburg's Voodoo Love God), was bred by Mary Rodgers of Marienburg Dobermans. He is a playful, entertaining member of Rita's family who enjoys his loving, sweet, and charming personality. Rita shows Voodoo in conformation, and he is close to finishing his championship. You can e-mail Rita at ta2d@comcast.net.

Kent Akselsen (www.akselsen.com) and Nikki Riggsbee (www.mcemn.com) share their home with several champion Great Danes. After many years of photographing Danes, Kent expanded his photography interests to include all breeds of purebred dogs as well as small animals and birds. His photographs have appeared in a variety of books, magazines, and calendars.

Jim Arnold is an equine and pet photographer whose work can be enjoyed at www.jarnoldphoto.com. The income earned from breeding an annual litter of vizsla pups is earmarked for his nine-year-old niece's college education.

Arlene Bishop is an avid dog fancier and trainer as well as a retired professional photographer. Arlene currently assists as a trainer with her local dog club and is training two of her own dogs for obedience, agility, and freestyle dancing. She travels with a portable studio, which allows her to indulge in her photography passion.

Karen Booth is an avid reader, amateur photographer, and lifelong lover of animals and nature. Karen lives in Minnesota with her housemate and their flat-coated retrievers. Even though they train and compete in several dog sports, the flat-coats are primarily beloved companions. You can visit Karen at www.wabanaflatcoats.com, view photos at www.flickr.com/photos/wabanafcr, or e-mail her at wabana@evensongfcr.com.

Jori Butler was born and raised in New Mexico where she still lives along with her husband, their three children, and a menagerie of four-legged friends. She is a long-time photographer who has a great love for nature and all that it encompasses. Jori's work can be viewed at www.cowgirllogic.com.

Jody Cohen is a volunteer with the Mid-Atlantic Great Dane Rescue League, Inc., and owner of Thankful Paws Donation Coats and Apparel (www.thankfulpaws.com). Jody rescued her Great Dane, Aspen, as a puppy. Aspen was abandoned in a park. Although Aspen is deaf and visually impaired, she has learned over thirty hand signals, has been a Great Dane Rescue Ambassador since puppyhood, and brightens the day of residents at assisted-living facilities.

Hayley Evans has a passion for animals and enjoys wildlife and pet photography.

Sharon P. Fibelkorn is a freelance photojournalist known for her keen eye and refined editorial work. She specializes in action photography. Her photographs have added visual illustration to most of the top publications throughout the world, both as editorial content and advertising. But it's those intimate portraits that grace personal homes and barns that have a special place in her soul. To say she simply enjoys taking pictures isn't enough. To say she has enjoyed her journey in life while creating and living moments with her subjects would be more accurate.

Shaina Fishman is a commercial photographer, specializing in animal portraiture, based in New York City. When not photographing dogs and cats in the studio or donating her time and talent to various animal shelters, she can be found spending time with her papillon, Cosmo. To learn more about Shaina's work, visit www.shainafishman.com.

Zachary Folk, based in Seattle, Washington, specializes in portrait photography. His online galleries include samples of his photos of dogs, children, and business headshots. Zachary also maintains a photoblog to organize his travel photography and daily shootings. You can e-mail Zachary at zachary@folkphotography.com or visit his website at www.folkphotography.com.

Donnie Gilpin is an award-winning photographer whose work has appeared in *The Finishing Touch, Eternal Puppy*, and *Just Terriers* magazine. His photographs capture the true personality of each subject in a unique and often humorous fashion. Bull terriers and his wife, Debbie, are the loves of his life and have served as delightful models for his photographs.

Stephanie Longinotti is a retired schoolteacher with a love for all animals, especially dogs and horses. After the loss of two other goldens, just three weeks apart, Stephanie was blessed to welcome Jack into her life. Jack keeps her young and active and is working hard to become a certified therapy dog.

Kelly Nechuta lives in northern Wisconsin with her husband, Mike, dog Cody, cat Charlie, bird Lucky, and Mr. Blue 2 the fish. Kelly enjoys outdoor activities, gardening, and quilting. Dog sports have recently become a great source of fun. She participates in obedience, agility, and hunt test training with Cody. They are entering their first hunt test this summer.

Natalie Rowe is a graphic designer, illustrator, and fibre artist living on an eighty-six-acre farm with her husband, two dogs, two cats, and a gecko, all of whom she enjoys photographing. Sophie (featured in the photo) and her brother were adopted by Natalie after their owner tragically committed suicide. Sophie understands French and English, loves snow, and adores fetching balls. Visit Natalie on her website: http://www.grinninggeckodesign.com.

Laurie Winslow Sargent is an author specializing in family play—including play with her four-year-old miniature American Eskimo mix, Nikki. Nikki loves soccer (catching the ball in the air with her front paws, dribbling, and blocking on command) and bounce-passing a basketball. She wipes her feet on a mat (for a treat!) and hops into her crate when she hears the AOL "Good-bye!" Best of all, when her family returns from work or school, Nikki greets them with an excited "Hi!" The sound initially occurred as a yawn that, coincidentally, sounded exactly like the word. You can visit Laurie at her website, www.ParentChildPlay.com.

Pat Shannon, the husband of coauthor Mikkel Becker and proud Pappa to two pugs, Willy and Bruce, is a junior at Washington State University in Pullman, Washington. An amateur photographer, Pat was on vacation in St. John, United States Virgin Islands, when he spotted Lilly, sitting relaxed in the sun, on a deck overlooking the bay. Pat grabbed his camera, Lilly shot him a canine Zoolander pose, and the dancing, liquid-filled eyes of this rover-rescue found their way to this book's cover.

Troy Snow is a professional freelance photographer whose work has been widely appreciated and published. Along with a team from Best Friends, he went to the Gulf Coast in the aftermath of Hurricane Katrina to help animals and people. The stories from that rescue effort are told in stunning photos in the book *Not Left Behind: Rescuing the Pets of New Orleans*. Many of Snow's photographs are on the Best Friends website (www.bestfriends.org), and you can see more of his work at www.troysnowphoto.com.

Maggie Swanson, a freelance illustrator of over one hundred children's books, lives in Connecticut with her husband, Rick, and two exceptional cats, Tommie and Gracie. She volunteers at PAWS animal shelter, and many of her photographs are of cats who passed through the shelter on their way to new homes. You can enjoy her work at www.maggieswanson.com.

TD Yandt hopes to positively impact the lives of pets and their people by creating great memories and teaching pet parents how to more effectively communicate with their furry family member. Meet TD online at one of her websites, http://noselicks.com (training information and tips) or http://caninecaptures.com (dog photography).

The Authors

Marty Becker, D.V.M., is the regularly featured vet on *Good Morning America*, a frequent veterinary contributor to *The Martha Stewart Show,* and the host of the PBS series *The Pet Doctor with Marty Becker,* which airs in hundreds of markets nationwide. He co-authored the *New York Times* bestseller *Why Do Dogs Drink Out of the Toilet?* and *Chicken Soup for the Dog Lover's Soul.* He has appeared on Animal Planet and writes a syndicated pet-care feature for newspapers across America and Canada, syndicated through Universal Press. Often called "America's Veterinarian," he has been named Companion Animal Veterinarian of the Year by the Delta Society and the American Veterinary Medical Association. Dr. Becker lives in Bonners Ferry, Idaho.

Gina Spadafori is the author of an award-winning weekly column on pets and their care, which is syndicated through Universal Press. She is a bestselling author of several pet books, which have sold 375,000 copies combined, including the *New York Times* bestseller *Why Do Dogs Drink Out of the Toilet?* and *Dogs for Dummies.* The first edition of *Dogs for Dummies* received the President's Award for the best writing on dogs by the Dog Writers Association of America. She has served on the board of directors for both the Cat Writers Association of America and the Dog Writers Association of America. Gina lives in Sacramento, California.

Carol Kline is a freelance writer and speaker and the bestselling coauthor of five books in the Chicken Soup for the Soul series, including *Chicken Soup for the Cat Lover's Soul* and *Chicken Soup for the Dog Lover's Soul,* as well as other books on a variety of topics. An animal rescue volunteer for years, Carol is affiliated with Noah's Ark Animal Foundation in Fairfield, Iowa.

Mikkel Becker received her degree in intercultural communications from Washington State University. Mikkel has been active in the Quarter Horse show circuit, and she is a three time Canadian National Champion in Western Pleasure and Hunter Under Saddle. Mikkel is a contributing author to Knight Ridder newspapers, *Cat Fancy* magazine, and Chicken Soup for the Soul.

Copyright Credits

(continued from page ii)

Index

Ears evocative of a butterfly's wings
give the papillion its name.

Jasper, a rescued dog,
enjoys his new life in
a loving home.

If you're not sure about something, hiding is always a good idea.

THE END